Enjoy these **PRIMROSE U.S.M.C.** titles from
R. Michael Haigwood

First Tour - Rescue
Second Tour - Suitcase
Third Tour - Sleeper Cell
Finders Keepers
Gilt
Squall

The cover shows the statue of Themis the Ancient Greek Goddess of justice
on the Legislative Council Building in Hong Kong.

In the Name of Justice

R. Michael Haigwood

Printed in the United States of America

First Printing November 2021

ISBN 978-1-956661-05-7 Paperback

ISBN 978-1-956661-06-4 Hardcover

ISBN 978-1-956661-07-1 eBook

Published by: Book Services
                www.BookServices.us

Contents

1. The Beginning. 1
2. The First Shot. 9
3. The Escape 37
4. The Gun Store 63
5. The Tribunal Council. 71
6. The File. 79
7. The Team 93
8. Details 105
9. Port of Tyre 119
10. Boarding Party 145
11. The Great Mosque. 161
12. Auf Wiedersehen 181
13. Site Prep 199
14. High Tide. 211
15. The Deluge. 221
About the Author 241

In the Name of Justice

Thanks to those who gave inspiration for the characters:

Robert J. Nakonieczny, USMC

Michael J. Nakonieczny, USMC

Thomas P. (Mad Dog) Naughton, USMC

H. C. Bowden, USMC

T. J. Martinez, USMC

Two Case Chapman, USMC

Harold Davidson, USN

Gary Kruegar, USN

Ronni Sullivan, Civilian

Gus (Sweet Freddie) Fuson, American Indian

In the Name of Justice

"Capitalism is the unequal distribution of wealth.
Socialism is the equal distribution of poverty."
Winston Churchill

Chapter One

The Beginning

Ten years old and scrawny, Quintin Underwood Michaels stood on the railroad bridge above the Palouse River, remembering the words of the playground bully the day before. Intent on scaring his smaller classmate, the bully had described in gruesome detail the accident that had broken a kid's neck when he had jumped into the river downstream at Granite Point.

Quintin looked down at his dad, his mom, his brothers, and sisters sitting on the small sandy beach, watching as he braved the heights of the bridge. His heart pounded in his ears as he prepared to jump into the lazy meandering river below. He was determined to stare down his fear and show them that he had what it took. There was doubt in their minds that Quint, the youngest of five, had the guts to jump. His brother, two years his senior, teased, "What's the problem, cry-baby? You chicken?"

His brother's taunt ignited the courage that Quint had hoped would come to the rescue. With the same inner strength he would call on time and again later in life, he grew past the gutless little ten year old in an instant as the barrier of fear shrank to insignificance in relation to the humiliation of being called chicken.

1

Finally, with all the enthusiasm of someone getting an appendectomy, he threw his body off the bridge. As he sailed through the air, he was thinking he'd never reach the water, and if he did, he would die on impact. In reality, the bridge was only ten or fifteen feet above the water. Even so, it was a long way down for a scared, underweight little ten year old.

When Quint hit the river, his feet split the water like a pro, leaving little or no splash. The entry was by no means planned. The beautiful jump was purely dumb-ass luck.

When he surfaced, the whole family was standing on the small strand of beach, clapping wildly for the little boy who, for the first time in his short life, had impressed somebody. As he swam to shore, his oldest sister met him with a towel and remarked, "You know Quintin, that was a damn foolish thing to do!"

Jumping off that railroad bridge was his first attempt at flying. Things looked a little different when he stood on the rear ramp of a C-130 turboprop thousands of feet in the air, getting ready to jump into the the inky blackness, hoping to land in the area designated on the map. It was a HALO jump—High Altitude Low Opening. He'd leave the plane, free-fall for thousands of feet, and then pop the chute just in time to avoid killing himself on impact. That was the easy part. After a safe landing, finding his target was always the real test.

The dreams faded away, going wherever dreams go, to be forgotten until they returned uninvited, and Quint rolled over to the aroma of freshly brewed coffee filling the flat.

The timer on the coffee pot had preformed perfectly. How did civilizations get along without such conveniences in the past, Quint wondered.

Today wasn't going to be just like any other day. It never was for a man or woman in his profession. This day would find the local paper's late edition splashed with news and photos of a nefarious individual reportedly responsible for the murder of two CEOs. He would be found with a hole in the center of his forehead, his death execution style. The man had bragged about shooting the capitalist pigs while he remained at large. Interpol couldn't find him, the FBI and CIA had not a sniff of his whereabouts. That's where Quint came in.

Quintin Underwood Michaels, shooter extraordinaire. To the few people he associated with and his family—Quint.

The dreams came back once or twice a week. They ranged from the skinny ten-year-old jumping off a railroad bridge in the middle of Washington State to the big kid jumping out of airplanes from the United States to Kathmandu.

3

Quint had tried to enlist in the Marine Corps after graduating from high school, but he was turned down as physically unqualified. The medical examiner suggested he was too frail to be of any use, and remarked that if he turned sideways, he would be invisible.

The shock of the rejection inspired Quint to take action: a regimen of weightlifting, martial arts, mountain climbing, and long-distance running. Within two years he had put on fifty pounds and grown three inches, peaking out at six-feet, 190, green and brown.

College held no interest. Firearms and marksmanship were his first love, and he was accepted as an apprentice in a rifle shop under a master gunsmith and expert marksman. With his tutelage, Quint became a master gunsmith and an expert with rifle and pistol. Shooting came to him as naturally as water to a duck, and it wasn't long before the student surpassed the teacher.

Quint's mentor had been a sniper in World War II and Korea. His tales of adventure kept Quint on the edge of his seat whenever he could get the old man to share his past.

In the rear of the shop was a hidden room Quint was not allowed to enter during the first year of his apprenticeship. When Quint had demonstrated that he had every intention of continuing with the trade and was well on his way to becoming a journeyman, the gunsmith granted Quint the privilege of entering his secret life.

Chapter One
The Beginning

The room was a maze of exotic weapons. Quint's mentor didn't question his customers, he just produced the weapons as ordered. The array of requests for his handmade tools of the trade was astounding. It was Quint's introduction into black ops worldwide.

With the privilege of working in the special shop came the introduction to odd characters from around the world. Most of the men Quint met contracted themselves out to governments, corporations, gangsters, dictators, and any number of organizations on the dark side of justice and injustice.

Most of their work never reached the papers across the globe unless the target was a high-profile individual like the head of a government or corporation. There was a huge discrepancy between the number of weapons produced and the news stories that should have hit the front page from their use. The lack of coverage was staggering when you considered that any event could be reported worldwide in a matter of minutes.

As Quint met these adventurers, an idea began to take root. He wanted to become one of them. As they entered the shop to collect their special projects, he would pump them for information. Some would share, some not. They were mostly a closemouthed, elite group that lived in a dangerous world. One slip of the tongue could mean the end of the hunt where they were concerned.

Quint's mentor finally told him to stop probing the clients. It wasn't good for business. He suggested that if Quint wanted to find a place in their world, he could introduce him to the right people. That was the beginning of a long and exciting career.

Quint finally gave in to the smell of the coffee and threw the covers back to begin the day in a rain-soaked villa by the sea.

The view from the balcony was spectacular on any day, and the storm hammering the coastline made it even more so. The weather made it impossible to finish the research needed to bring down the bragging killer of CEOs, but it would clear up soon, and the killer would get his reward—a round entering his demented brain.

The wind was blowing the rain and salt water from the waves against what passed for a picture window. Quint sat and sipped his coffee. The patter of the rain was almost hypnotic, and he slipped into images from the past. He could see the rifle range clearly. He was lying in the prone position on the thousand yard line, hitting the black with every round as the contract warrior John Ash looked over his shoulder nodding approval. John was testing Quint for a small job he'd contracted with a two-bit wannabe dictator in Central America. On the recommendation of Quint's mentor, Ash had agreed to introduce Quint to his clandestine world.

The contract was to eliminate the wannabe's opposition, who otherwise would most likely win the upcoming election by a landslide. Because both the wannabe and his nemesis were lowlife cockroaches, John had agreed to do the job. What the wannabe dictator didn't know was that as John Ash took him out, Quint would be taking out the opposition. The world would be a better place without them.

As it turned out, they eliminated the competition for another commie asshole standing in the wings, who took over the country.

The job paid well, and with the new president in place, it wouldn't take long for another wannabe to require their services. It was pure job security.

It was Quint's introduction into what John Ash called *In the Name of Justice*. He would only take jobs where the bad guys lose. He was a warrior for justice. Unfortunately, he was killed in an automobile accident pursing a bad guy in Iran.

With the rain still pounding the window, the irritating sound of the phone interrupted Quint's travel into the past.

"Quint here."

"Quint, the man you want will be at the Oxygen Bar on the corner near the local smoke shop at ten in the morning."

The phone clicked before Quint had a chance to get more information.

He slammed the receiver down, regretting he hadn't found a more reliable information source. The guy on the other end was a flaky SOB, untrustworthy regardless of the amount of money paid for his supposed loyalty. He was afraid of his own shadow, but the smell of green gave him enough courage to stick his neck out just enough to get by. When the danger made him sweat more than the smell of green gave him false courage, he would disappear along with his fee.

Because of the weather, Quint thought the day would be a bust, but one never knows when opportunity will knock.

Chapter Two

The First Shot

They exited the taxi and headed for the ticket window through the scurrying throng. The flight had a little more than an hour before departure. Quint sat down in the row of empty seats and watched John Ash talking with the ticket agent.

John was taking a chance with Quint on the recommendation of Quint's mentor, who had requested that John introduce Quint to his secret world.

John Ash, known in his world as Jack, was a man of average appearance, more like a school teacher than a figure in the clandestine world of those whose trade was death. A muscular five ten with brown, twinkly eyes, his light brown hair was cut in an Ivy League style to match his professorial glasses. His posture was unassuming, enabling him to easily blend in with a crowd. Well-trained in the martial arts, he'd been a member of a special group that worked for the National Security Agency. His knowledge of who the bad guys were around the globe was a never-ending resource for the work he took on from various world leaders and international organizations when he retired from the NSA after twenty years of service to his country,

With tickets in hand, he turned and motioned for Quint to follow him to the boarding gate. They would sit separately on the plane, and when they arrived at their destination, they would travel as individuals to the hotel. Two gringos traveling together would send up red flags to anyone looking for a hint of trouble. People in the business knew what to look for and kept a sharp eye out to prevent problems for their bosses.

Quint was a long way from Blaine, Washington, a town on the border of the United States and Canada. The Peace Arch in his home town advertised the peaceful relations between the two countries. On farms along the border, you wouldn't know which country you were in as you strolled through the miles of unprotected woods.

Growing up there was like growing up in any rural town in America, except that Blaine was on the main highway from Mexico to Vancouver, Canada. But even with the freeway, it kept its small-town flavor, with a small fishing fleet in the harbor along with the private yachts and cabin cruisers. The border was peaceful, the only sign of its presence the long line of cars on either side.

Beyond farming and fishing there was little to keep young people from seeking greener pastures. Farmwork, school, and church kept them busy and out of trouble until they were old enough to seek their fortune in the world.

The gun store kept Quint occupied after school and on weekends, and it had led to his present situation. From Blaine to Central America in a few short years was more than he'd hoped for.

As the plane made its descent through the cloud cover, the city came into view, sitting in a maze of thick, green, impenetrable jungle. The plane slowed, the tarmac came up to meet the wheels, and a little puff of smoke arose from the tires as it touched down.

Quint looked back down the rows of seats to see Jack folding a daily paper as he stood to retrieve his carry-on from the overhead compartment. Jack caught his eye, nodded, and shrugged his shoulders towards the exit.

Quint was nearly the last one to deplane. Jack was already walking towards the baggage claim area in the small airport.

Heavily-armed soldiers guarded every entrance and exit, each one with a stack of posters that he referred to regularly. Jack stopped to talk with one of the soldiers. Quint felt a rapid increase in his heartbeat as he watched Jack and the soldier look through the posters. Then, after a chat and a short handshake, Jack proceeded towards the baggage claim.

When Quint's pulse returned to something approaching normal, he presented his baggage claim ticket to a young man who would be called a skycap in the States. He quickly retrieved Quint's single bag. Jack had claimed his baggage already and was heading for the taxi stand to catch a ride to the hotel.

The only decent hotel was full of gringos. Most of the visitors were trying to suck up to the anticipated victor in the upcoming elections. They presented any number of schemes to enhance the bottom lines of their companies. Jack and Quint would not be out of place in the crowded hotel.

After checking in to different rooms, they met in the restaurant for lunch. The place was full, so they could sit together and not attract any unwarranted attention.

Jack kept his voice low. "I'm supposed to meet a woman here this evening. She'll have the information we need to take care of business. After lunch we'll stroll down the street to a local cigar store. The proprietor is a friend who will have the weapons we need. I shipped them down some time ago, when I first got the contract. We've done business before when I've been in this part of the world. He is reliable, but very expensive. I know him only as José."

Quint was constantly amazed at the professionalism of Jack and his connections. Everywhere they went he hooked up with someone to assist him.

After they finished lunch, Jack retrieved a large cigar from his jacket pocket. Lighting the huge stogie, he remarked, "Time to go see José. He'll appreciate seeing me smoking one of the cigars he sent me for Christmas. They come from Havana and are quite pricey. The last box he sent was from Castro's own selection. Speaking of the old dictator, word is his days are numbered. His health and the ambitions of his brother may end his tenure."

The sidewalks were crowded with noontime shoppers, effectively camouflaging their short walk to the cigar store. They didn't stand out in the bee-hive of activity. "I think with the election coming up people are anticipating trouble and are on a spree to stock up on essential goods in case the country goes haywire with curfews and martial law. Unknown to them, the candidate will not be around to get the vote, and neither will his opposition. The wannabe dictator has plans to eliminate the candidates so he can move in, declare the country under siege, and install his communist government," explained Jack, as they made their way through the crowded street.

"But he won't succeed, for he'll not be around to implement his evil plan," he added as they turned into the cigar store.

As Quint followed Jack into the store, he was impressed at the technology involved in making an ordinary-looking building on the outside look like a huge cigar humidor on the inside. The place was wall-to-wall cigars, displayed in their origi-nal wooden boxes. If there were any cigar makers not represented, they were either out of business or they'd been taken over by bigger companies.

A chubby, cheerful, roly-poly guy, José sported a huge black mustache that framed the sides of his mouth and twisted at the tips, held in place with wax. His teeth were dark yellow from constant exposure to his Cuban cigars.

"Hello, my friend Jack. I have been expecting you. Who is this young fellow?"

José wasn't pleased to be dealing with anyone but Jack and made no bones about it. "Jack, our deals have always been one-on-one. I'm not comfortable with new faces."

"Not to worry, José; this is my apprentice, Quint. He's honorable, reliable, trustworthy in any situation, and willing to go the extra yard to take care of business. You can be sure he'll watch your back as well as mine."

José kept staring at Quint, not so sure about the newcomer.

Quint kept his eyes locked on the cigar-chewing proprietor and smiled. "José, it's nice to meet you. Jack has good words about you and your business of selling the best cigars on the planet. I'm looking forward to a long and rewarding friendship." He extended his hand.

José mellowed a little. He shook Quint's hand in a firm grip to seal the friendly, if skeptical, introduction. He was not much on change, for his was a dangerous world. One mistake could mean the end of both his business and his plan to enjoy a long life. He looked at Jack, searching for any insincerity on his face. Finding none, he shrugged his shoulders and turned towards the rear of the store.

Jack and Quint followed, but José disappeared before they could get around the counter. As they stood in the back of the store looking around, the wall spun and José appeared from behind the rotating storage shelves. He smiled and said, "Okay, gentlemen, please follow me."

They followed as José rotated the wall back into place. The opposite side was dimly lighted by one exposed bulb hanging from the ceiling. Just below the lone bulb a flight of stairs led down to the basement. They descended the stairs, José flipped a switch, and the room lit up like a department store. There was merchandise of every kind for people in their profession. He walked over to a large workbench and pulled a long box from under the far end. It had the markings of a UPS delivery made sometime the month before. "Here, my friend, is the box you sent. As far as I can see it's intact. It was not intercepted by the government police or customs." He smiled and chuckled, "They allow me to receive things without inspection for a small annual fee."

Jack opened the box. It contained two rifles, scopes, night vision goggles, special ammo, and silencers. "Thanks, José. Everything seems to be here. We'll want some other things, but I'm sure you can help us with what we need."

"Anything for you, my friend," responded José.

After Jack and Quint finished assembling their equipment, Jack said, "Okay, José, we'll leave our stuff here for now. We have a dinner meeting with our employer's representative this evening. If we need any further assistance from you personally or for equipment, it will be determined in that meeting."

José nodded, and after checking the monitor to see that no one was in the shop, he opened the well-hidden opening to his secret shop and storage room.

Jack and Quint shook hands with their host and departed the cigar store grateful to have such a reliable connection in a country on the verge of deciding whether to accept the will of the voters or surrender to anarchy.

At the appointed hour, Jack and Quint entered the hotel restaurant to find the table they had reserved occupied by a young, attractive woman. Not knowing who would be there to meet with them, they were pleasantly surprised. Not many women that young were entrusted with such an important message.

When they approached the table, the young woman stood and extended her hand. "Hello, Mr. Ash, my name is Hilda."

Jack took her hand. "Hello, Hilda. This my associate, Quint."

Quint grew weak in the knees from Hilda's radiant smile. He extended his hand, but for the first time in his life he was tongue-tied. He just nodded and felt like a fool.

Hilda shook his hand longer than necessary and gave a little squeeze as she released his grip. Quint hadn't realized how firm his grip had been, but she didn't seem offended by his lapse of manners.

Jack noticed the lingering handshake, along with the eye contact between the two young people. He hoped it didn't spell trouble. They didn't need any distractions in the pursuit of the mission at hand. Breaking the spell between the two, he said, "Shall we be seated and get down to business?"

Hilda, a little red-faced, said, "Gentlemen, as you know, I have been sent to give you the itinerary of your target." She spoke in a low voice.

Jake leaned toward her. His Spanish wasn't the best, and Quint was of no use, staring at her totally enamored.

"Hilda," he said, "you need to slow down and speak up a little." She spoke up a little.

"We don't know who is watching or listening. I have to be quick about this meeting and be on my way." She handed Jack a thick envelope.

Jack put the envelope in his jacket pocket and gave her a menu.

Quint finally came out of his fog, found his voice, and spoke up. "Hilda, do you have time for dinner?"

"Regretfully I do not, but a cup of coffee would be nice." she said.

After the waiter took their order and Hilda had her coffee in hand, she remarked, "After you have studied the contents of the envelope, call the number at the bottom and I'll give you the rest of the information you need.

"My boss is skittish about this plan and wants to make sure you follow his instructions. He doesn't trust anyone he didn't grow up with. My leader is surrounded by his boyhood friends and neighbors, me included."

She glanced at Quint, then looked pointedly at Jack. "He was also under the impression you worked alone. I doubt he'll be happy when I report that you are not alone, and you're not following the plan you outlined for him."

Not intimidated for a second, Jack said, "Hilda, Quint is my apprentice. He's an asset to the operation, especially with the rough jungle terrain you have down here. I have worked here before, and two are better than one. He's well-trained and, as you can see, very fit."

"I'll relay your thoughts to the boss, but he'll still not be happy. He doesn't like change, except in the government he's about to take over."

Hilda appeared to be a die-hard follower of the wannabe dictator; she would bear watching. Jack said, "Tell him there is no cause for alarm. The job will be completed as planned; his money will have been well spent."

Hilda finished her coffee and stood, saying, "I must get back to my people. I'll expect a call early tomorrow."

Before they could stand to be polite, she turned and disappeared out the restaurant entrance and down the crowded street.

"Well, Quint, she sure made your usual rapid-fire flow of words about anything in general come to a complete stop."

Quint was slow to reply, "Was she the most beautiful woman you have ever laid your eyes on or what?"

"Do you think because she has green eyes, blond hair, and a figure that would put Marilyn Monroe to shame—not forgetting a smile that could melt an icecap and the fact that she was also taken with you—that's some kind of qualification for you to get wacky on me? Bullshit! We don't need any complications. Get her out of your head, both of them!" said Jack, as they began to eat the meal the waiter had just deposited on the table.

Jack stopped chewing and continued, "Listen, when we're finished here, we'll be on her shitlist. The best thing you can do is suck it up and concentrate on the mission. You know with that blond hair she sticks out like a redwood in the Mojave Desert."

"I get the point, Jack. I'll keep my mind and body into the task at hand." With dinner finished, they retreated up to their room to discover what was inside the envelope.

Jack peeled back the flap and retrieved the contents. He laid everything on the desk for a close inspection. There were pictures of their mark standing on a huge stage among his faithful—not a big man, early fifties, glasses, potbelly. There were clippings of him in different locations.

The bottom page was a map with instructions to be followed the next morning. They were to wait in the lobby for Hilda to come and pick them up. She would guide them to a small village in the jungle, where they would pick up another envelope that contained the location of the target and the times he'd be vulnerable. Hilda would stay with them throughout the mission and make the final payment for their services when the hit was finished.

Jack remarked, "I don't like the way things are going. We can't do any recon and make sure of our position. According to the timetable for the wannabe, we'll barely arrive at the site in time to set up. We'll not have a safety net for retreat if things go bad or an escape route to disappear after the hit. Piss-poor planning means piss-poor performance and maybe even failure."

Jack dialed the number at the bottom of the page. He was surprised to hear Hilda answer, "Yes Jack. What can I do for you?"

Jack responded, "I don't like the setup. I can't do the hit without a recon of the whole area. In order to protect myself and Quint, I'll need to check out the area a day before to be sure we have a safe environment; otherwise you can tell your boss to get someone else."

After a long pause, Hilda came back on the line. "Jack, I'll lead you out there tomorrow morning, and you can do as you want. He has two meetings planned. You can hit him on the second meeting, the following day. Anything else?"

Jack said, "See you in the morning," and hung up.

"Quint, I think we can use the magnetism you have with Hilda to find out where her boss is so we can take him out after he pays us for doing his opposition. Both these guys are scumbags of the first order. We need to watch our backs on this one."

"Good morning, gentlemen," Hilda said as she approached them in the hotel lobby. "Shall we go? I have a jeep waiting out front. It's not far. The jungle gets really thick once we leave town and get off the main road."

Quint sat in front with Hilda, with Jack in the back keeping an eye on their six. He had a feeling they would not be alone. There was something fishy going on, but he couldn't put his finger on it.

As he listened to Hilda and Quint chatting about nothing in particular, he wondered how such a beautiful, charismatic woman got herself mixed up with a group of communists who would all die sooner or later, hunted down by whatever government was in charge at any given time.

She was right on. The ride was short. She stopped on a hill overlooking a small valley, where there was a stage set up in the manner of an outdoor theater.

"That's where he'll be giving his speech tomorrow afternoon. He usually speaks for an hour," Hilda said.

Jack and Quint spent the next two hours going over the area, charting their best options for arriving and departing. They chose the best spot to take the shot and avoid being discovered. It would be hard for the departed's friends to know where the round came from. The initial confusion would give them enough time to make their way out of the area.

With the recon finished, Jack suggested, "Let's head back to town and have lunch."

While they were having lunch, Jack said, "We'll need a jeep or something with four-wheel drive."

"It's all arranged. There'll be a jeep parked in front of the hotel in the morning. I'll leave the keys at the front desk." As they got up to leave the table, Hilda said, "Quint, I have a party to attend this evening. Would you like to join me?"

Quint was surprised by the invitation, but quickly answered, "It would be my pleasure to escort you. Yes!"

"Good then. I'll pick you up around seven."

With that, Hilda got up and left the hotel without looking back.

The following morning Jack asked over breakfast, "Well, how was your date, young man?"

Quint pondered the question for longer than Jack thought necessary. He prodded the younger man, "Come on, Quint, let's hear about the party."

Quint whispered across the table. "When we finish eating, let's take a walk where no one can possibly overhear us."

"What's with all the cloak-and-dagger shit, Quint?"

Quint retorted, "Jack, when we get outside, listen to what I have to say with a keen ear. Hilda is not what she seems to be. We are damn lucky she was sent to us instead of another one of those commie fuckers."

With breakfast finished, Quint followed Jack out the front door of the hotel. After the two men had walked a ways down the sidewalk, Quint said, "Hilda is not what she presented to us at our first meeting. The party we went to last night was for her and our employer. The difference between Hilda and us is, shall we say, not much. Her loyalties do not lie with the wannabe dictator. Hilda is a double agent for the opposition presidential candidate, who is likely to win by a landside if he isn't assassinated. Her job was to infiltrate the wannabe's organization and inform the good guys what was up. Hilda's real boss didn't know there were two different factions fighting to take him out. She also didn't know we were going to take them both out and let the people decide who would lead their country.

"It's a damn good thing she was the one chosen to help us, because there's a sniper team on the opposite side of the valley ready to kill you after you take the shot on the wannabe. That way they can blame the killing on the hired gun of the evil Americans. Then they assassinate her real boss, who is a clear choice to win the presidential race. Voila! The new wannabe steps in and takes over the country. You are dead and the U.S. gets the blame for the whole mess."

"Jesus, how the hell did she get mixed up in all this?" asked Jack.

Quint was trying not to get too excited about what he'd learned and talk too loud in the crowded street. He said, "Her father was a German diplomat with the embassy, and she fell in love with the country. From her diplomatic ties, she met some high-level government people and stayed on after her family returned to Germany. When the last president was taken out, she vowed to stay on and help the real government take back control and institute free elections. She's a real idealist.

"She was approached by the current party running for office to snuggle up to the opposition so they would be forewarned of any trouble. She fell in with the wannabe dictator and gained his confidence. Lucky for us, once again. The reason she shared her story was because she knew we were not bad guys and that we actually wanted both of the wannabes out of the picture, which was her goal.

"They don't know there are two of us. She has the itineraries of both the bad guys and is willing to share the information so we can bring them both down at the same time. The country will blame the deaths on a long-standing feud between the two rival rebel factions.

"Hilda thought you could do one and me the other—problem solved."

Jack had been on some unusual operations before, but this one was taking the cake. "I don't suppose with you and Hilda it was love at first sight? She had a lot of guts to share her information with a complete stranger. She's in a very ticklish position. One mistake, and it's curtains for her. Where is she now?"

"There's a bar on the next block where we meet her. If we show up, she knows we are willing to help. If we don't, she figures we're on our way out of the country."

Jack was beginning to like the intrigue. "Let's go meet with Hilda. I would like to help this country and do the world a favor. Yes, let's go with our original plan and take them both out. But we can't do it at the same time. You'll have to take the snipers who intend to do me. Then we take out our paymaster."

Jack felt the hair start to rise on his neck. "You know, Quint, this all sounds a little too pat. How do you know she's not running a scam on you? You don't know her from owl shit!"

They had reached the bar and were turning in as Quint answered, "You'll know when you talk with her that she's on the square."

Entering the bar after walking in from the bright sunlight presented a situation no one in their line of business wanted to be in—they couldn't see!

Because this wasn't their first rodeo, when they entered the doorway, Jack stepped to one side and Quint to the other, both taking the nearest chair. Removing their shades and turning their backs to the wall, they waited until their eyes adjusted to the dark interior of the saloon.

It didn't take long before they could see Hilda waving for them to come to her table near the rear door, where she handed them a manila envelope with passport pictures of the intended targets. She seemed agitated as she whispered, "We have a problem."

Jack looked into her eyes, observing her facial expressions. He was as struck by her beauty as Quint was, but also by her words. Maybe she was on the square after all.

Her voice soft and quiet, Hilda said, "Jack, your target has moved his schedule up, and Quint, your target will be coming into this establishment around four this afternoon. I don't know how you can cover Jack and be back here on time."

Jack replied, "Not a problem. The people who are supposed to snipe me think I'm going to be in the place you set up, right?"

"Yes," Hilda responded.

"Not a problem. I'll get there early and take out the snipers first, then my prime target. Quint can take care of his business at about the same time. We'll be back at the hotel before they realize what's up.

"I guess you know, Hilda, they're going to put two and two together and figure they have a huge leak. They'll eventually get around to checking on who knew what, and when. You'll be a prime suspect."

Hilda didn't blink. She said, "I spoke to the presidential candidate, and he suggested I take a vacation starting tomorrow. If you don't mind I'll tag along with you on the flight back to the States. He knows the danger I'm in, but after the elections he'll have the power to arrest all the scumbags who are working for the two rivals."

"Hilda, is there anyone in your circle of friends that you're not sure of?"

"Not that I'm aware of, no."

"Okay, we'll head back out the front and return to the hotel to prepare for this afternoon."

Hilda responded, "I'm going to slip out the back. I'll be at the hotel later this evening. If things get out of hand, I can have a jeep to take us south. There is a private airfield a few miles inland, but not something you'd want to use unless it was the last straw. The old

27

man who owns the field has two vintage airplanes. He would rent us one. Can either of you pilot a plane?"

Jack smiled. "Flying is a hobby of mine. Yes, I can fly most anything I can start."

Hilda smiled, stood up, and was out the rear door before either one of them could get to their feet.

"I'm okay with Hilda. I think she's on the square. You're right, Quint, she's passionate about this country and its future. Let's head back to the hotel and get this show on the road."

Back at the hotel, Quint was incredulous. "After all the firearms training and dragging all the high-dollar equipment down here, you want me to use *this* to kill the asshole?"

"Quint, you can use this and be out the door before anyone even knows what happened. You go in there blazing away with a handgun or an automatic rifle, and you'll not see the sun set. Your target will have twenty bodyguards around him. You can't kill them all without some return fire and one hell of a nasty international incident if you get wounded and captured. I've used this blowgun on numerous occasions. It's perfect for you today. You *have* practiced with one before, right?"

"Yeah, sure, they were around the store. We used to sit and try to hit a bull's-eye on the wall when we weren't busy. I can use it just fine. I didn't know you'd brought one along."

Jack placed the blowgun on the table and retrieved the little bottle of poison from his bag. "Just dip the arrow in the bottle for a second and try to hit his neck. He'll be dead in seconds, and out the door you go. It's so dark in there, no one will see you."

"You know, Jack, you sound like the seconds in the corner of the ring, watching the fighter getting his ass kicked. They keep telling him what a great job he's doing, and he's wondering what the hell fight they're watching."

Jack smiled, removed the blowgun from the table and said, "Since I've used this before, let's do it this way. I'll take care of the wannabe in the bar, and you take care of the target in the jungle. I think you can handle the situation. Now let's get moving. You have to be there early enough to eliminate your would-be bushwhackers."

Quint was sitting across the valley looking through his binoculars at the two would-be snipers. They looked like Abbott and Costello during their heyday. It was amusing to watch them try to camouflage their sniper position, obvious that their training was limited. It appeared that whoever trained them didn't want them to be too good, so if things turned around they wouldn't be shooting back at the trainer with any accuracy.

When they had completed setting up their position, another soldier appeared out of nowhere and began chewing them out for some reason or another. When he departed, they argued between themselves, which gave Quint the opportunity he needed. With two quick shots he ended their disagreement. The thick jungle muffled the sound of the rifle, and after waiting for a few minutes Quint decided no one had heard the shots.

Picking up the brass from the two rounds, Quint slipped into the overgrown vegetation and found his way to the spot he'd picked to take the shot that really mattered. It was near time for the wannabe dictator to show up with his entourage. He'd have plenty of bodyguards around him, but that wouldn't help him see the next sunrise. One round would end his career as a would-be tyrant. He wouldn't be running his country into the ground with empty promises to the poor and defiance to those who would help bring the country into the civilized world.

As Quint was getting comfortable in the sniping position, a pebble bounced off the leaves just to his front. Looking around, he couldn't see or hear anything, so he rolled out of his position and disappeared into the green foliage.

Jack, seeing Quint's reaction to the pebble, was pleased to see his student had the sense to disappear. He whispered, "Quint, it's me, Jack. My target had a change of plans, so I've come to give you a hand."

"Jesus Jack! You scared the shit out of me."

"Sorry Quint, I didn't know any other way to get your attention without getting myself killed."

Quint slipped back into his sniping position. As Jack crawled in from the opposite side, the wannabe dictator and his guards arrived at the jungle clearing. Their vehicles, painted with green camouflage, had been nearly invisible as they approached. As they came to a halt, soldiers appeared out of the jungle from the north. They'd been waiting for him to arrive before revealing themselves.

"Quint, it's a good thing we decided to pick a position from the south, or we would've walked right into the mouth of the lion."

Jack looked through his binoculars as he continued. "The main guy is in the lead vehicle sitting shotgun. You can take the shot whenever you're ready. He seems to be waiting to dismount for some reason."

It was put up or shut up time for Quint. He could sense Jack lying next to him, watching his every move, his every breath, as he fed him information on the target and surroundings.

As he prepared to shoot, Quint heard Jack whisper, "You might want to ponder your decision because this shot will determine your life's path."

Quint squeezed the trigger and felt the recoil as the bullet left the barrel. He knew the round would find its intended target and rid the world of a butchering psychopath. The victim was the perpetrator of unspeakable crimes against all who opposed him. He would not fulfill his ambition to take over the small country as his personal playground and killing field. How these maniacs could convince a whole population to follow them was a mystery. Maybe fear was the motivation—follow or die!

Jack, still looking through the spotting scope, reported, "You hit the target in the right temple. He was on his way to hell before he fell out of the vehicle. Good shooting. The door has just slammed shut behind you, my friend: you are now on someone's most-wanted list. He has friends who'll be looking for the man who disposed of their leader. Let's take our leave of this position before they figure out where the round came from."

Crawling away from their sniping position, Quint had mixed feelings about the shot. He was excited to finally use his skills on a target that mattered; but he felt a speck of guilt. The guilt didn't last long as he remembered the pages of offenses the would-be dictator had committed against his country. He was the enemy of all mankind, not just his country of origin—good riddance to him.

Quint cleared his head and followed Jack back the way they'd come. When they were far enough away to not be heard, Jack asked, "How did you do with the two who were sent to snipe us?"

"They were not a problem. Poorly trained—for good reason I suppose, since these people seem to change loyalty with the wind. The world has three fewer bad guys scavenging society. What about your guy, what's up with him?"

"Hilda came into the bar as I was doing a recon to find the best seating position to make the hit. She said he was delayed four hours, which means we have a little time to return and get set up."

As they neared their vehicles, the sound of mass confusion could be heard coming from the clearing. Automatic gunfire sprayed in every direction as the soldiers shot blindly into the foliage. The jungle behind them was filling with soldiers who were in danger of getting killed from friendly fire as they fanned out to look for the shooter that had killed their leader.

As they got to their vehicles Jack asked, "Where did you get the car?"

Quint, who was nearly out of breath responded, "I borrowed it from in front of the hotel. It was just sitting there with the keys in the ignition. I thought I'd leave it a block from the hotel when I was finished with it."

"Shit man, leave it here. It'll throw them off."

"Hilda left this jeep for us to head south if things went bad. Jump in, let's get the hell out of here!"

The front entrance to the bar was deserted except for a couple of skinny dogs fighting over a bone. The street was narrow with high curbs to keep the rainwater from entering the businesses along the short block of adobe brick buildings. They drove the jeep around to the rear door and backed it in. There was a good chance they'd be in one hell of a hurry when they hit the door.

"Bring your grease gun, but keep it hidden," Jack told Quint as they jumped out of the jeep.

It was dark as ever inside as Jack led Quint to the table he'd chosen earlier. A few patrons were scattered about at the tables, and the bar itself was nearly half full.

Sitting down with their backs to the wall, Jack said, "Our eyes should be adjusted to the darkness by the time our target arrives. He's supposed to make a short speech from the stage there. It's just the right distance for a clear and accurate shot with the blowgun. He won't know what hit him, and those around him won't figure it out right away. It should give us time to vamoose."

Quint thought about it for a minute and inquired, "Not to bring up bad possibilities, but what if you miss?"

Jack was not surprised by the question; the kid was catching on fast. "If I miss, which is highly unlikely, you'll have to shoot the SOB and most of those around him with a full magazine from your grease gun, as we take our leave as quickly as possible. In the event that happens, Hilda's jeep and her promise of a plane to lease if we head south will be on our agenda. How many magazines do you have?"

"Just two, and I hope we don't have to use them. Our surprise will have a limited time until they open fire in every direction. Then it's 'oh well' for those in the line of fire."

In the Name of Justice

Chapter Three

The Escape

While Jack and Quint were discussing their options, Hilda came through the front entrance with a throng of loyal supporters of the wannabe dictator. The group spread out, taking seats at the tables and bar. Hilda didn't appear to see them at first. As she became accustomed to the darkness she looked in their direction but didn't show any sign of recognition. She took a seat close to the stage.

Quint nudged Jack and said, "Hilda is too close to the stage. If something goes wrong, she'll be right in the line of fire. We need to speak to her somehow and let her know what's going to take place. She needs to know what to do if things don't go as planned."

Jack thought about the situation for a few minutes. "Quint, I'll walk by her table on the way to the banos and nod for her to follow me. I'll go into the hombre side. Once there, I'll explain the situation and make sure she moves out of the way when our target begins to speak."

"Don't forget to tell her the jeep is in the rear and that she should head for it during the confusion," reminded Quint as Jack got up to make his way towards Hilda's table.

As Quint watched, Jack passed Hilda's table and nodded towards the banos. She got to her feet and followed him.

They were back in no time, and Hilda chose a different table closer to the rear exit.

Before Jack had taken his seat, the wannabe dictator came through the front door with his cadre of bodyguards. The arrogant little prick was so short he disappeared in the center of his entourage. Waving his hands like a recently elected politician, he jumped up onto the stage, where he turned and faced the throng of the faithful.

He spoke so rapidly it was hard to keep up with his ranting. His faced became flushed as the speech took on a life of its own. The body gestures, arm waving, and snarly facial expressions made it a prize for a *Saturday Night Live* segment.

Jack had the blowgun hidden inside his shirt. He pulled a small bottle of poison and a dart from his pocket. He dipped the dart into the end of the bottle and soaked the tip with the lethal liquid. With that done, he returned the bottle to his shirt pocket and retrieved the short blowgun from inside his shirt; he was ready to take the speaker out.

Quint was amazed at Jack's steady hand and patience in such a sticky situation. Things could go bad in a second, and he acted like he was playing bridge.

Jack sent the dart on to its destination. It hit the speaker in the nose just below his right eye. As he put his hand up to the dart, gunfire sprayed the inside of the saloon. It took a moment for the poison to take effect, giving him time jump off the stage and head for the rear. He collapsed near the door from the poison and from the thud of many rounds hitting him in the back.

The attackers were soldiers loyal to the wannabe dictator who was now pushing up daisies in the jungle clearing. It had not taken them long to lay the blame for his demise on the rival wannabe's group.

The rear door was clogged with bodies, and the only way out was to blast through the front entrance. Jack motioned for Quint to spray the front with the grease gun to make a hole for them to take their leave.

Quint pulled the trigger as they rushed the entrance, hitting everyone in their path inside and outside. The ones who dodged the bullets scattered in all directions.

Jack turned his back to Quint's to cover their six and fired away with his handgun. As they reached the door, Hilda could be seen coming up the street in the jeep. She screeched to a halt on the opposite side of the narrow street and waved them to hurry up.

As they approached the jeep, she jumped over into the shotgun seat, and Quint took the wheel.

Spinning the tires after popping the clutch, Quint pressed hard on the accelerator, hoping to put some distance between them and the chaos behind them.

Hilda yelled over the noise from the motor and gunfire, "Head south."

Quint was doing just that when a large truck pulled into the street ahead of them, blocking their departure. It was a government vehicle, and there were troops in the bed aiming their rifles at them. Quint stopped the jeep about fifty yards from the truck and looked in surprise at Hilda.

Hilda jumped out of the jeep and approached the government truck, yelling at them to let her pass as she waved her government credentials at them. One of the soldiers jumped out of the cab as Hilda got closer. He checked her identification and immediately arrested and cuffed her.

Quint pulled the jeep up to the scene, and Jack jumped out, demanding an explanation. The soldier said there was an arrest warrant out on her for conspiracy to topple the government.

Hilda turned pale and then suddenly shoved the soldier and grabbed the handcuff keys.

Quint used his last magazine to spray the truck as Jack and Hilda jumped into the jeep. Jack took the wheel and Hilda jumped into the back seat. Quint, now out of bullets, took the shotgun side as Jack backed up and spun a one-eighty to head back towards the bar. Hilda yelled for him to take the first right and then a left to put them on a course for the main highway heading south.

Quint looked back as they turned the corner. The rebels had arrived and were engaging the the government soldiers in a fierce firefight. The battle would keep the opposing forces occupied for a while, which would give them time to make their getaway without any interference.

As they tried to keep their balance in the speeding jeep, Hilda gave Quint the keys to remove her handcuffs. She said, "I think the government was using me to keep tabs on the rebels. I can't believe the president would use me like that. I was a believer in his policies and loyal to the cause. I hope you guys got paid in advance; we'll need the money. The old man and his planes are a hundred miles south, straight ahead. I think my best bet is to fly out with you. My naivete has nearly gotten me killed."

Jack turned to Hilda. "You have been betrayed by someone. Who knew where you were today?"

Hilda frowned, her lips pressed tight as she thought about the question. Before she could answer, Jack remarked, "Jesus, who the hell surveyed this road? They must have been smoking the local weed."

It was all Jack could do to keep the jeep on the road and make any time. They had a hundred miles to go, and it wouldn't be long before the confusion behind them would turn to anger. When that happened, there would be a posse on their ass.

Hilda finally answered Jack's question. "I have a very close friend who knew my schedule, but she would only reveal it if she was tortured. I can't imagine why they would even question her. She was not part of the government. They must have had surveillance teams on everyone who worked for the president in a clandestine position."

After four hours of hard driving, the sun had disappeared into the ocean, and they hadn't gone more than fifty miles on the serpentine road.

Quint and Hilda were trying to doze a little in the bouncing, swaying jeep as Jack maneuvered it around one pothole after another.

After another couple of hours, Jack pulled the jeep to the side of the road and asked Quint, "Well, how are your driving skills in the dark of night on a treacherous road, my friend?"

Quint took the wheel as they kept the jeep heading south.

It was near daylight when the jeep crossed another of the many bridges on the road. As they passed over it, Hilda shouted, "Up over the next rise we'll be able to see the airstrip in the dale below."

Quint, with a look of skepticism, asked, "How the hell do you know that? It's pitch black. You can't see forty feet in front of the jeep."

"There are markings on the bridge abutments. That bridge was the last one before the road climbs up over a ridge. Down below will be the airstrip and a village."

Jack remarked, "I hope they don't have phone service, police, or soldiers in the area."

Hilda replied, "There was phone service last time I was here. The village has a small police force, and there are military troops just outside the town. The army troops are from the area, so they aren't very aggressive."

As the jeep neared the crest of the ridge, Quint spotted a side road, steered the jeep into it, and parked it under some low-hanging foliage.

They dismounted and began to camouflage the jeep. It would be their second option if the plane thing didn't work out.

Jack said, "Hilda, as soon as it gets light, Quint and I are going to recon the field and the village. You stay here until we return."

Hilda, unhappy with the thought of being alone, said, "I would like go along."

Jack fired back, "You stay here and think of this jeep as your lifeline. If we're not back by noon, you take the jeep, head for the nearest border and go directly to the American embassy. Case closed!

Hilda started to resist the orders, but the look on Jack's face told her to take his advice, so she climbed into the driver's side and retrieved a set of binoculars she had brought along for the trip south. "You might want these," she said.

Jack accepted the binoculars with an apologetic smile and a warm thank-you. They would be invaluable during their recon.

When the sun decided to show itself over the mountainous jungle, Quint climbed to the top of the ridge and looked through the binoculars at the small airfield. There was no activity from the hangar or the airstrip. The village was beginning to show some life, but it appeared there weren't any alarms being sounded.

They couldn't see the army garrison located further south from the village. They would have to take a look there before trying for the airfield. If there were warnings sent out to expect a trio of gringos, it would present major problems. Hilda was still upset about being left behind, but between Jack and Quint they convinced her that it was best she wait with the jeep until they returned.

With Hilda wishing them Godspeed, they began the journey down into the valley. The foliage was thick until they reached the edge of the valley floor, where they stayed in the jungle to conceal themselves. They wanted to find the army post first thing and observe it for any signs of alarm.

Jack was scanning the area just to their front when he caught a glimpse of the army post buildings. "There it is, Quint. Not even a guard visible. There should be lots of activity this time of day.

Let's scout the perimeter, in case we need to make a sudden retreat."

As they made their way around, it was apparent the post was completely deserted.

Quint stopped and pointed out the headquarters building. "Look, the doors are open."

Jack stood up and said, "Fuck it. Let's walk right into the HQ building and see if we can find out why this place seems to be abandoned. There have to be phones, note pads, bulletin boards, orders lying around–something."

When they entered the building, it looked like any other military office. Desks, phones, stacks of paperwork in the in and out boxes. The country's flag was draped on the wall, along with the current president's picture. The commander's office was directly to the rear.

Jack entered the CO's office first, searching for anything that would give them a hint as to where the troops were. As he entered the office the phone clanged for attention. He hesitated before picking up the receiver. In his best Spanish, he said, "Capitán Martinez."

Quint could hear the party on the other end from his position standing in the office doorway. Jack kept nodding and saying, "Si'."

After a five-minute conversation, Jack replaced the receiver. "Well, we don't have to wonder what the hell is going on. That was some major from

God-knows-where. He said the complete garrison is at the airfield, and that I was to call their CO to inform him that the three gringos had made it out of the country. How we did that is yet to be determined. Anyway, he said to also tell the CO to gather his troops and return to the post.

"The problem we have now is the airfield guy will be scared shitless to help us. With the smell of the army still in the air, he won't be so enthused about us showing up and wanting a plane. We better head back to the jeep, get Hilda, and bring her with us. She knows the guy, so we'll let her make the deal. He might be more comfortable with her. We're getting a plane ride, with or without his consent. He can take the money and smile or find himself tied up with no money and no airplane." Jack, seeing the airfield number on a note pad, rang the field and relayed the message for the commanding officer to return to the garrison.

They retraced their steps back to the jeep. Getting out of the country was becoming a challenge.

With the jeep in sight, Jack whispered to Quint, "We better check out the area before just walking up to the jeep and Hilda. Someone might have discovered her and the jeep."

After their recon, they found the jeep untouched, but no Hilda. "Damn! Do you think she took off by herself? Maybe she was abducted!" declared Jack.

Quint shrugged his shoulders. "I don't see any signs of a struggle," he said. "I think she would have put up a furious battle before giving in. No, I think she took off to who knows where."

Jack started taking the branches off the jeep. "Let's get the jeep on the road and head for the airstrip. We don't have a clue where the hell Hilda went, and it won't be long before the local army will discover they've been duped. We need to try and make a deal for one of the planes and get the hell out of here."

Quint agreed. He jumped behind the wheel, fired up the engine, put it in reverse, and backed out, slowing down just enough for Jack to hop in.

Backtracking, they found the road that led to the airfield. With the army on its way back to its post, Quint felt no need to be cautious. He opened up the jeep whenever the terrain allowed, and it didn't take long to find the end of the airstrip.

It was short and looked more like a cow pasture than something smooth enough to take off from. The grass had been allowed to grow knee high from end to end, and Jack was not smiling. "I think even if we find a decent airplane, this so-called runway will put my skills to the test."

Quint stopped the jeep two hundred yards from what looked like the old man's office building. Next to that was a single hangar and a fuel pump. The whole scene looked like a horror movie set with the monster about to stake his claim.

Jack said, "What the hell! Quint, take us right up to the old building. What have we to lose?"

Quint put the jeep in first, but released the clutch a little too quickly, so it jumped, spinning its wheels in the soft sand of the old road. At just that moment, a plane could be seen coming out of the single hangar, taxiing towards the head of the overgrown cow-pasture runway, getting ready for takeoff.

"Jesus, Quint, hurry the fuck up. Somebody is stealing our plane."

Quint floored the gas pedal, and the jeep spurted to top speed in second gear. Before he could shift into third, they were within spitting distance of the plane. To their surprise, Hilda and the old timer who owned the airfield could be seen at the controls of the little four seater.

As the jeep pulled up to the plane, the engine sputtered and died. The old man had shut the engine down, and the plane rolled to a stop.

Hilda jumped out and yelled, "We don't have much time. I made a deal with the old man. Sorry about leaving the jeep, but I knew you'd be back and not have much time to dick around. I could see the soldiers heading back to their post. And then the old man got a call from the soldiers telling him to watch out for the gringos, because someone had fooled them into returning to their garrison. He wants his payment in Yankee dollars."

Jack immediately climbed down from the jeep and began to inspect the airplane, shaking his head as he ran his hands over the antique. "Quint, we might be taking a chance with this old bird. Of course, there's the other option—facing a shitload of soldiers who don't like us and are armed to the teeth—the president's army and two rebel armies who frown upon their leaders being dusted."

Quint was admiring Hilda's beauty as she stood beside the plane, smiling, waiting for them to make a decision. She had taken the initiative and provided them with the transportation they needed to escape.

"Hilda, we need the plane to get the hell out of here. We can tie the old guy up and leave him in the office, to cover his ass with the soldiers. Where does he want us to send the money?"

"He gave me an account number for a bank in San Jose, Costa Rica. You can make a deposit for him there. His sister lives nearby, and he'll be heading that way soon. The government has condemned the airfield property and will give him less than half of what it's worth. He can take their offer or find himself in prison—or dead."

The old guy was listening and seemed to understand every word. He started towards his office.

Jack had finished checking the plane out. "Quint, you guys take him to the office and tie him up while I get this antique started and ready for takeoff. We don't have much time, so be quick about it."

With the old guy tied and gagged, Hilda and Quint ran back out to the old field, only to find Jack having a hard time getting the plane running. He was swearing up a storm, and by the sound of the cranking, the battery was getting low.

When they were all in the plane, he gasped, "One more shot. If she doesn't start, I think we're in for some serious shit." As he gave it another try, the sound of vehicles could be heard in the distance. The army was on its way back.

The engine sputtered, coughed, and began to run as the army vehicles came out of the jungle at the far end of the runway, heading straight for them. Jack yelled over the noise of the engine, "Hold on to your hats."

Jack throttled the engine up, and when it was at the right RPM he began to taxi towards the head of the runway for takeoff.

The engine sputtered and died. "Shit" was all Jack could say.

The army trucks, loaded with soldiers, were bearing down on them. Little spurts of dust could be seen around the plane, but also around their trucks. They came to a sudden stop, and the soldiers jumped to the ground for cover. They were taking gunfire from the edge of the runway.

Hilda yelled, "It's the rebels!"

Quint added, "This may be our opportunity to make it out of here. Give it another try, Jack!"

Jack responded, "Well, the short run may have charged things up enough." He gave it another go. It sputtered again, but caught. The engine began to hum like it had just been tuned up. With the throttle pulled to the max, the plane took off down the so-called runway and skimmed over the first trucks as gunfire riddled the wings and tail section, the bullets passing through the thin skin of the craft. The rebels and the soldiers forgot about their battle, and all guns were shooting at the plane as it left the ground, barely missing the tall jungle trees.

After clearing the trees, Jack brought the plane around and set a course for Costa Rica.

With the course set, they all began to relax and wipe the sweat from their faces.

Hilda remarked, "Damn! That was a close call."

Jack responded, "Don't get complacent. The fuel gauge is not showing full. Hilda, did you fill the tanks?"

"Yes, the old man and I topped off the tanks before he fired her up."

Jack frowned. "I think a stray round may have vented the fuel tank, but the gauge doesn't seem to be dropping too fast. With a little luck we'll be able to find an open space to set this relic down. It may have been destiny for us to have a hole in the tank, giving us the incentive to land as soon as possible, instead of waiting for the rivets to pull apart and send us to the jungle floor."

Quint was searching the green below for a spot long enough to bring the airship down when Hilda yelled, "Look to the left! There's a huge open field!"

Jack banked the plane to get a better look as the engine began to sputter again and without fanfare stopped. "Shit, here we go again. We'll have to glide down to the field. I hope we're over the border."

Jack tried to coax the engine back to life, but it was a no-go. Forgetting about a restart, he concentrated on bringing the plane down safely, which he did without incident, swearing to never get himself into such a situation again. He had allowed things to get out of hand, which was not good for a guy in his line of work.

As the plane bounced to a stop, four men on horseback rode up and asked if they could help.

Hilda spoke first. "Yes. Could you tell us where we are?"

The one who seemed to be the leader responded, "Yes. You're in Belize."

Hilda sighed with thankfulness. "Would it be a problem to give us a ride to the nearest commercial airport?"

The leader spoke. "I'll call for a truck to come out, take you to town, and tow the airplane to the ranch. We have a mechanic there who might be able to help you."

Quint could see the events of the past as clear as day. He looked out at the wind and rain pelting the bay window. That was the last time he'd seen the beautiful Hilda alive. Her picture made the front page of a newspaper some years later; she was lying in the street after being shot at a political rally. She'd not given up on her quest to bring freedom to the people of Central America.

Jack had sold the plane to the rancher who helped them, and they'd caught a commercial flight back to Washington State. Quint's first adventure into Jack's world had been a learning experience, to say the least.

Shaking the past out of his head, Quint started getting his gear together. He needed to be at the Oxygen Bar to dispatch the scumbag to the hell he deserved. Killing CEOs in the name of communism was like robbing a bank and dividing up the money, only to realize the bank was now empty and no more funds would be available. You don't kill your source. It takes capitalism's money to support the socialist-communist ideals. It was a no-brainer: no free market, no income, no socialism. Socialism's all-inclusive style of living couldn't support itself—it would eventually crumble from within.

Quint would set up his firing position nearly two blocks away and would be gone before anyone could determine where the round had come from, if they ever did. The bullet would hit the murderer between the eyes, just above the bridge of his ugly nose.

Quint put all the equipment he would need in his travel bag and taking one last look at the surf washing onto the beach, decided he would retire soon. He wasn't tired of taking the bad guys to the cleaners, but he longed to try living a normal life. He'd thought about it often, and then the words of John

Ash would come to him: *"You might want to ponder your decision, for this shot will determine you're life's path."* John had said that when Quint took his first shot in the name of justice. From that day forward he'd pulled the trigger many times. There was a laundry list of scandalous regimes that had put a bounty on his head without knowing who he was or what he looked like. Many of their lackeys had been sent out to discover his identity, but without success.

Quint always kept his promise to Jack that he would, without fail, be sure his target was as advertised. Being the executioner was the heaviest of responsibilities, and he didn't take it lightly. Each case was treated with the utmost care. The individuals or organizations who requested his services were investigated along with their targets. Ninety percent of those who inquired about his skills were rejected.

With so many out there trying to identify him and take him out, it didn't leave much room for a so-called normal life, so once again he just shined those thoughts on. He shut and locked the door and turned into the driving rain, hoping it would let up a little for the shot that would take out the bragging assassin of innocent people.

It was only a couple of blocks to his previously selected firing position, so Quint decided to walk and not have a car to worry about. It would be easier to just disappear into a coffee house or a lunch counter.

The streets were not crowded as Quint walked down the sidewalk. The few shoppers were inside the stores avoiding the rain. The weather was supposed to clear up in the early evening, which was good for Quint, because the streets would be crowded when he finished his business and walked away.

Turning into the alley in the second block, Quint made his way to the fire escape and climbed up to the top of the five-story building. The roof was one huge puddle of water. Whoever designed the building was not a master of his craft. Splashing his way to the far end of the roof and looking out over the street, he could see the Oxygen Bar on the corner two blocks down the main drag.

He set his tools of the trade down on the only dry spot to be found, which happened to be a huge hooded cooling fan. Pulling the binoculars from the bag, he stepped over to the edge of the roof railing and scanned the Oxygen Bar. It was crowded with those seeking to fill their bloodstream with pure oxygen from the colored glass tubes filled with water that served as a humidifier.

His target had not yet arrived, so Quint spent a lot of time watching the street and taking everything and everyone into consideration in case he had to make a fast departure.

The rain had become a light mist, which wouldn't disturb his shot much. It would even muffle the slight noise from the rifle as it expelled the deadly projectile that would end the life of a confessed murderer. His trial, conviction, and sentence would be carried out in the few seconds it took for the bullet to hit its mark. Bingo, one less terrorist for the world to deal with.

Because the halls of justice moved too slowly for today's fast-moving international world of terrorism, it had become necessary for individuals and organizations to take the initiative. Those were the words Quint would hear over and over again, as his skills were retained by one or the other. The terrorist knew no boundaries, be it nation states or individuals. The notion that they only killed in the name of religion was just so much bunk. They were plain criminals, pure and simple, killing in the name of their insane ideals or for the ideals of another zealot.

The suicide murderers were of another cloth. They were indoctrinated from birth to die for their leaders under the promise that they would find rewards beyond belief for their sacrifice. Yet it was clear to even the casual observer that their leaders never set the example. It was also interesting that they would give their lives to kill others, and their opponents would give their lives to save lives.

After another look at the street leading to the Oxygen Bar, Quint focused on the bar itself. The place had gained a few more oxygen freaks, but not the evil one whose time had run out. Leaning back against the fan hood, he began to assemble his weapon, remembering the care his mentor had always taken, treating the weapon like it was a beautiful woman, to be caressed and pampered, touched softly and held firmly so it would explode when the time was right.

Disassembling the rifle would take but a few seconds once he took the shot, and he'd be on his way. Speed was important only until he reached the street, where he would blend in, just another shopper.

Drying off the binoculars for another look at the bar, Quint discovered it had gained additional patrons and was crowded to the point of overflowing out the door. That was not a good sign. His target would be hard to pick out, let alone hit, in the mass of flesh trying to pay for something that was free to anyone who wanted to step outside and take a breath.

Returning to his position against the fan hood, Quint went through the ritual of calming his system before the storm. He'd learned over the years to become one with the surroundings. Nothing could disturb his total commitment to the mission.

After the short ritual, Quint felt the tension leave his body and a deep sense of placidity overcome any nervousness that might cause problems when he pulled the trigger.

Picking up the binoculars, he again wiped the mist off the lenses and searched the bar for his target. It had thinned out a little as people took their hit of oxygen and departed.

Luck was on Quint's side. His target walked in front of the binoculars just as he was going to set them aside and wait awhile.

The evil shooter of innocent people was about to draw his exit visa. He looked as advertised: short, a little overweight, with the undeniable trait that set him apart from others—his full head of red hair. It was quite a contrast, the olive dark skin and the red hair. There must be some Irish blood in the loud-mouth.

The braggart sat down at the bar, and while the attendant was putting the oxygen mask on his face, a man ran into the center of the store. Quint could only see his profile, but his lips were moving in a manner suggesting panic.

Quint put down the binoculars and picked up his rifle. He positioned the rifle scope on the figure standing in the middle of the shop. He was still yelling something at the people taking oxygen. Moving over to his left, Quint focused his sights on the one whose life expectancy was getting shorter by the second. In his photo he wasn't nearly as ugly as in real life.

Quint put the scope hairs right above the man's nose and in the middle of his forehead. The bullet would hit there and expand as it entered, not going clean through and hitting an unintended innocent target.

Little beads of sweat began to form on Quint's forehead, and along with the thick mist from the rain, the scope was beginning to fog as he pulled the trigger.

The bullet struck its target as intended at about the same time as the guy who ran into the shop opened his shirt to expose the device wrapped around his waist. Quint pulled the rifle away from his shoulder just in time to see the Oxygen Bar disappear, along with most of the building and all the windows for blocks around. The explosion could be felt for miles.

Quint was in no hurry to put his tools away, as the streets would be full of emergency personnel, police, and rubberneckers after the terrific explosion.

Because of the confusion in the streets, the walk back to his digs was without the usual circuitous route he would have taken to throw off anyone who might be following. It felt good not to feel the hair on his neck and arms getting stiff at every corner.

Once back at the oceanfront room, he dialed the number of his employer. The number from his phone would show up on the other end, and they would know it was him.

The voice on the other end responded harshly. "I don't think you needed to blow up the whole fucking block to kill one murderer. You may have caused an international incident, depending on what the investigation finds in the remains. Your track record doesn't show any such extreme measures. What the hell were you thinking?"

After listening to the dressing down, Quint responded, "Number one, I'm a little disappointed that you would think I was so stupid as to be responsible for such a blatant act. Number two, I terminated the target with one round between the eyes, just above the bridge of his ugly nose. I had no part in the explosion that rocked the building. I did see who pulled the trigger on the waist-mounted device. When the suicide bomber entered the shop, my target didn't flinch. It was as if he knew him or was not expecting any trouble. He felt safe in the Oxygen Bar environment. I'm heading for the airport, and I will be at my Washington number in a couple of days."

There was a long silence on the other end of the cell connection, with a lot of chatter in the background. Finally a single voice said, "We have a project on the board that will take all the skills you have acquired over the years. Actually it's two projects, but related. Take a couple of weeks off. We'll give you a call and set up a date to meet. This project can only be discussed face to face. Your normal fee will be renegotiated." The cell went blank.

Quint thought he might take on one more mission before hanging it up. He had bank accounts around the world with enough funds to live any lifestyle he chose for as long as he lived.

He pulled the curtain on the beachfront apartment, locked the door on the way out, and said goodbye to Casablanca.

Front page photos in the papers worldwide showed the Oxygen Bar before and after the explosion. More than one terrorist organization claimed responsibility for the attack. The word on the street was that there were two major players in their world meeting to join forces. A third party evidently didn't want the parties to join hands. The bragging killer who snuffed out the two internationally known CEOs was not mentioned and probably not even known about. There was nothing left inside to identify him. Quint just smiled—another job well done.

While Quint was sitting by the window seat in first class, he reminisced about the first contact he'd had with his employer.

The office was in an enormous underground complex near Sandia, New Mexico. He'd had to go through seemingly endless checkpoints manned by civilian security to get there. He initially thought it was a government building. It turned out to be anything but.

His first contact was with a pencil-neck office type, a Don Knotts look-alike, who gave him a folder to review while he cooled his heels in the waiting area. It explained little, but it piqued his interest. He'd been referred by John Ash to the cabal with the highest recommendation possible. Anything John had been associated with was okay with Quint.

The first meeting set in motion more than a decade of constant adventure. The past weeks had been taken up with just one of many assignments around the world. His work seldom made the papers, which was a good thing, because it kept his identity from Interpol, the FBI, the CIA, and any local or international police organizations. He could practice his trade without the burden of multiple identities, which usually became a liability, as keeping track of them was an open invitation for a life-ending mistake.

Chapter Four

The Gun Store

The plane landed at Sea-Tac International in Seattle, where Quint boarded the shuttle to Bellingham, a small college town on Puget Sound. From there he rented a car and returned to his roots in Blaine and to the old gun store where he'd discovered his calling.

The telegram had come weeks before. His first mentor and teacher had passed suddenly and left the store to him. Quint couldn't return immediately—too many urgent assignments—so he had hired a man to run the place until he found the time to come back and decide what to do with the business.

He entered the shop and announced who he was. The man running the shop came around the counter, extended his hand, and said, "Welcome home, Mr. Michaels."

Quint looked at the young man, raised an eyebrow, and remarked, "I was expecting a much older gentleman than you are! By your resume, I expected you to be near fifty."

The tall, lanky soft-spoken kid couldn't yet be in his thirties. His hair was bushy and unkempt, and his blue eyes smiled when he spoke. He looked every bit the circuit preacher from the Old West, whose thin frame could be seen for miles around on horse-back. His trimmed mustache arched as he smiled showing perfect white teeth.

"Mr. Michaels, I did exaggerate a little on my pro-file. Even though most was true, I felt it necessary to add a little fire, because I've run into the "you're-so young-looking" thing before, and it has hindered my employment."

Quint looked at Jake Dahl and decided not to make an issue of the fudged resume. The shop was doing very well on the bottom line. The kid seemed sincere and evidently was more than qualified to take care of business.

"Okay, Jake, all that aside, tell me why you wanted to run a gun store."

Jake was a soft, slow speaker, and even slower when speaking about himself. Quint felt like he had to draw every word from him. "Speak up, Jake, we're not in a library!"

"Well, Mr. Michaels—"

"Forget the mister shit, my name is Quint."

"Yes sir. Well there isn't much to tell. I grew up in Spokane. After high school, I attended two years of junior college and decided it wasn't for me. From there I joined the Navy to see the world. One thing led to another, and I was chosen for the Navy SEAL program. That's when I discovered what I wanted to do with my life. When it came time for firearms training, it was like a lightbulb lit up. When the first round left the rifle barrel, I knew that was my life's work.

"I spent eight years in the Navy; I was wounded a couple of times on special ops. The second time they decided it was severe enough to discharge me on a disability. So here I am, working with the tools that I enjoy. This is not a job for me, but an adventure. I'm like a kid going to the county fair. The days aren't long enough for me."

Quint could see how enthused Jake was. He was pleased he'd hired him.

Scanning Jake from head to toe, he could see no reason for the young man to be drawing disability. "Jake, what am I missing? You have all your limbs, and you don't limp. Why should my tax dollars be going to you?"

Jake smiled and in his slow manner of speaking explained, "I have only my right eye. I lost the other from shrapnel. The glass eye is almost a perfect match. I'm not bothered by it ninety percent of the time." Smiling again, he added, "As you know, scopes are not made for two eyes. I felt a need to be around weapons of any kind, and after being near or on the ocean for eight years, I wanted to be by the water. Thanks for giving me the opportunity."

Quint was impressed with Jake; his background might be an asset. He didn't reveal that he knew the kid had found the back room. With Jake's years in the SEAL program, he would understand the needs of someone in the field who was working under harsh, sometimes impossible, conditions. And he would understand what those conditions might demand in the way of weapons.

He decided to work with Jake for a while and get to know him better. Then he would decide whether or not he wanted to reveal his true profession. Who knew, maybe the kid would be interested in becoming an apprentice.

After a couple of quiet weeks working with Jake in the shop, Quint's special cell phone vibrated, announcing that the tranquility was about to end.

The voice was the same as always, a dry monotone with no face. Except for the first meeting, all business over the years had been by cell, telegram, mail, or landline.

The familiar voice suggested an in-person meeting for the first time in more than a decade. Recovering from his surprise, Quint realized that whatever was on the agenda, it must be way beyond anything he'd done in the past.

Quint tried to respond in the same monotone: "I need two more weeks. Can it wait?"

After a long silence; a voice Quint didn't recognize came on. "We have a time sensitive target, or should I say targets? Please come down to Sandia ASAP!"

Quint was intrigued now. Who the hell was on the phone, and why didn't he introduce himself?

He had wanted more time with Jake to be sure of him before giving Jake an opportunity to become his apprentice, but that was out the window.

"Jake, how long have you known about the room in the back of the shop?"

Jake looked a little startled at the question, and started to hedge around, but in the end, he decided to just tell the truth.

"Some time ago, maybe the third week. I found it the most fascinating place I've ever seen. I discovered it by accident, but once in there, I was mesmerized. It was then that I knew what I wanted to do with my future. I didn't tell you for fear you'd fire me."

Quint pondered Jake's response. "I have a security device that told me the room had been breached. Now that you know what I do and you seem to be inclined to be in the business, would you consider an apprentice position?"

Jake didn't quite know what to say. He'd expected to be fired for his intrusion. He replied, "Yes sir. I would be honored to follow in your footsteps. I did liberate a good portion of your personal records and found them captivating. I have been hoping that when you returned, we'd be having this conversation.

Quint looked into Jake's eyes, trying to find any doubt in his response. Not seeing any, he said, "Welcome aboard, and keep in mind you may withdraw at any time you feel uncomfortable with the direction you're going. Then again, you have to remember that once you pull the trigger, it will be difficult to return to a normal life. With luck you will not have your identity exposed; you must protect that at all cost."

With the partnership sealed, Quint went on to explain the call he'd taken earlier. "That call means something big is in the wind. I'll have to take a trip to New Mexico and find out what's up. I'll be back in a couple of days. In the meantime, you take care of the shop, and I'll keep in touch. You might further study some of my case histories to get some firsthand knowledge of how I operate. We'll need to be on the same page at all times. If ever we are not working from the same mindset, one or both of us will die."

Jake sat behind the counter while Quint was on the phone to the airlines. This was not a fantasy anymore, but the real thing. All his visions of being a world traveler and defender of justice were about to materialize, even though some might consider the way they meted out justice was criminal. Fact is, they would only shoot those who had earned the right to die for their crimes.

It was like football: when you broke the rules the referee penalized you. He was the judge, jury and enforcer. If you didn't break the rules, there was no penalty. The difference was that football was a game and the world was deadass serious—no crime, no penalty.

Quint put the receiver to the wall phone back in its cradle and said, "I have a flight in the morning. I'll drive down to Seattle tonight and take care of some business, so I won't have to fight the traffic in the morning. You hold down the fort, and I'll call when I know something."

After Quint left the shop for Seattle, Jake's cell phone buzzed. He flipped it open. The voice on the other end came through loud and clear. "Did he buy it?"

Jake was surprised; the plan had been to wait for two months and then report.

"Yes, he bought it hook, line and sinker. I'm in," responded Jake.

The voice asked, "Did he share anything about his employer or his next target?"

Jake felt a twinge of annoyance. He'd only been with Quint for a couple of weeks, not near enough time to discover all the workings of his operation.

"No, he hasn't confided in me about anything except for his war room, and an invitation to be his apprentice. I've not been around him long enough to ask pertinent questions. He's left for a meeting somewhere in New Mexico, and he'll check in when he can. In the meantime I'll go through as many of his papers as I can."

The voice continued, relentless with questions Jake couldn't answer. "Look, pal, I can't tell you any more than I have. What the hell is the rush?" responded

Jake with more than a little heat in his voice. These guys may be paying his fee, but they didn't own him.

The voice came back, "There is something brewing in his world, which means our world. Whatever is going on, it has international consequences. We may have to step up the program considerably. I'll get back to you."

The cell went dark, which was okay with Jake. The guy was a first class asshole anyway.

Jake closed the shop for the weekend to concentrate on Quint's files. There were two huge filing cabinets nearly the length of the hidden room's back wall, and they held the history of Quint's adventures.

With two days to go through the files, Jake began his research with the latest file and worked backwards. Quint was the most professional individual he'd ever run across. His attention to detail was phenomenal. Over the years he had made zero mistakes. The more Jake read, the more respect he had for Quint. Too bad they weren't on the same team. There was so much to learn from Quint, but sadly they were on opposite sides of the termination business.

Jake's job was to find out as much as possible about Quint and his associates and then terminate them.

Chapter Five

The Tribunal Council

All representatives had found their chairs and were seated at the round table, when the first speaker rose to address the group, whose members were not known to the general public.

"Ladies and gentlemen," the speaker began, with all the enthusiasm of a death row inmate taking his last few steps to the electric chair.

"This emergency meeting has been called because of a problem on the horizon. It seems our many enemies are conspiring to join forces to destabilize the free world and bring down the global stock markets. Their objective is to disrupt the daily lives of all who enjoy freedom. We have to nip this new offensive in the bud.

"One of our main players is waiting in the reception room. He's been a loyal supporter of our efforts over the years and has performed with brilliance. He may be the key to dismantling this summit meeting of our opposition.

"Their summit meeting is scheduled for the first of next month. That gives us a little over two weeks to organize a response. I believe all we need to do is take out three of the leading antagonists, and the others will fold. The new players in the game don't have the stomach of the old guard."

The first speaker introduced the next speaker. "Hilda will fill in the details." He took his seat, and Hilda stood to address the gathering.

"Gentlemen, there will be nearly twenty attendees at this meeting. Each will represent a different terrorist group. In the past they have been so fragmented that it was impossible for them to mount any kind of joint effort. Today, almost every country around the world is on the alert, with some wanting to appease. Thank God there are others who want to be proactive and take the battle to the terrorists. Until the rest of the world gets the message, we'll have to take the lead. As we have in the past, we'll stay covert and act accordingly.

"The terrorists will be meeting in Tyre, Lebanon, a logical site, as it is centrally located for most of the attendees. A few will be coming from South and Central America.

"Inside the folders before you is our game plan for their summit. When we adjourn, please place the folders in the barrel at the door as you exit."

Cooling his heels outside the conference room, Quint was getting irritated. Numerous individuals had come and gone without acknowledging his presence.

Just as he was about to take his leave, a woman in her early twenties emerged from the meeting room. She was pleasant, but very matter of fact in her tone and manner.

"Sir, would you please follow me?"

She turned and headed back through the door. Quint was glad to be moving. From past experience, he knew what was awaiting him.

When Quint entered the room, all heads turned towards him. As he scanned the room, he saw only one familiar face. Considering that it had been years since his last face-to-face meeting, he was not surprised. But then his eyes landed on another familiar face. It belonged to a woman sitting near the twelve o'clock position at the round table. The last time he'd seen her was on the front page of a newspaper, lying dead in the street of a Central American city in the aftermath of a street riot.

When their eyes met, he could see the fire still burned within her. She showed no sign of recognition. His mind flashed back to their adventure in Central America and the hair-raising escape from Nicaragua to Belize. That was the last time he'd seen her alive. It was obvious the years had been good to her; she was still beautiful—for a dead person. Hilda and Jesus must have had the same recuperative powers.

Quint nodded to everyone and took a seat at the table. They all thumbed through their folders for about ten minutes. Without looking up, the person seated to his left asked, "Quint. May I call you Quint?

Sitting before the group of strangers, Quint was beginning to feel like a circus curiosity.

"Yes. Quint will do."

The question was just a delaying tactic while the man was thinking about what he'd learned from his folder. He appeared to be the youngest among the group, but had the posture of someone used to being in charge.

"Quint, we have a world class situation on the horizon. What can you tell us about it?"

Quint thought for a few moments and responded, "I only know what I've read in the report. Then again I don't need to know a whole lot about such things in my business. All I need are the histories of my targets and positive identification. And, of course, location and time schedules. The politics surrounding my assignment are not my concern. I just do in the bad guys who have it coming. I know what I do makes the world a better place. The dark side is an equal opportunity employer, and I just try to even the odds for the good that wars with evil in the world."

As Quint was speaking, he was looking into the eyes of the people seated around the table. He lingered a bit when he passed Hilda. She still didn't show any sign of recognition. "I wonder if she is a twin?" he thought.

The man was not pleased with the answer and passed on asking another. The others up to Hilda had no questions. It was a cinch they'd all read his history.

The cabal who hired his services had been formed to protect the interests of free people around the world. Their enemies knew no borders and had no limits in their wickedness, trying to drive the modern world back to the dark ages. It was a never ending battle, handed down from generation to generation.

Hilda asked, "Quint, you've read the contents of the folder. Is there enough information for you to take on the assignment?"

Quint looked at Hilda with questioning eyes and responded, "Yes."

"Good. Then we can count on this meeting of the terrorists to be a complete failure!"

"I don't know about a complete failure." said Quint. "But one thing for sure: they'll be minus three of their top leaders, as suggested."

"Thank you, Quint. Would you mind waiting in the lobby? We have some other business, and then I would like to speak with you in more detail about the mission."

Quint complied with the request and found his way back to the lobby, glad to be out of the stuffy chamber. He much preferred to do his business over the phone or by computer.

He had not been sitting long when the door from the chamber opened and the round table filed out, walking past him without notice.

Hilda was the last one through the door. Without stopping she signaled him to follow her. She headed down a long hallway. All the doors were generic, with only numbers visible to identify the occupants.

Hilda arrived at the door numbered 66, inserted a card, and the sound of the lock releasing could be heard. The door swung open to reveal a large room furnished with a feminine touch. She walked around to stand behind a large desk with a backdrop depicting a tropical waterfall.

Quint was the first to speak, "What the hell is going on here? I saw you on the front page of a newspaper some time ago, and you were quite dead!"

"It was necessary for me to disappear. I was in considerable trouble with a certain regime, and I had to get the heat off me. Being dead was as good a way as any. Soon after that incident, I found my way to this organization. For years now, I've followed your career with interest. No one here knows that we have a past. I thought it would be best to leave that alone."

Quint was watching Hilda closely, looking for any cracks in her armor. She'd been tough as nails during the hair-raising escape to Belize, but that was years ago.

Hilda opened a thick folder on her desk and thumbed through the first few pages.

"Quint, this is the detailed plan that was outlined in the other briefs handed out at the table today. I will give this one to you. It has the names, photos, history, and schedules of your targets. The terrorist meeting will be in a few weeks. If we can eliminate the names listed, we will disrupt their chain of command and leadership roles for years to come. It's not common knowledge, but these groups have joined hands with environmentalists around the world, along with the Communist and Socialist parties. We have to snip this quickly. As you know their target is capitalism and free societies around the world. Their agenda will not allow for religious freedom or for anything else that doesn't follow their interpretation of the book they follow. Those who won't oppose this surge can only hope they will be killed last."

Quint could see she still had the fire of her convictions. "Hilda, if I only have a few weeks to get the show on the road, I need to get started. Do you participate in any of the field operations?" he asked.

She responded with a quick smile and shook her head in the negative, "No, they won't let me out of the building. I would enjoy getting out there and participating in this one with you. I think it'll take more than one individual to bring down these targets. Do you have anyone working with you at present?"

Quint was not one to lay all his cards on the table. "Not at this time. You'd be welcome to join me."

Hilda looked a little startled at the quick invitation, but countered. "I'd like to get back out there and fight alongside you, but you'll need me here. I can be of more help to you with my hands-on information coming in from all around the world. I'll give you a number to call whenever you need information or a heads-up on what's going on far and wide. I'll be the only one to answer. If you'll give me a secure number, I won't call unless it's an emergency."

"Okay, Hilda, but the offer will remain open if you decide to reconsider it sometime down the road. For now, how about giving me the package you're looking at, and I can get started."

Hilda wrote her private number on the inside cover and handed the bulky file to Quint. "I wish you well, my friend. Call me if you need any help."

With the folder under his arm, Quint did an about-face and headed out the door. Looking down the long corridor, he was happy that this place wasn't the site of his life's work.

Returning to his rental car, he headed to the airport and his flight back to Sea-Tac. The information in the folder would require at least a week of intense study. He would begin on the plane ride home.

Using his cell phone, Quint dialed the number of the gun store, hoping to catch Jake before he closed for the evening.

"Gun shop."

Quint was glad to find him still working. "I'll be back in Seattle late tonight. I'll stay in town overnight and be in Blaine sometime tomorrow before dark. I have an assignment."

Chapter Six

The File

Jake didn't expect Quint to be back so soon, so he stayed up late and went through as many of the after-action reports as possible. He was amazed at the amount of work Quint had done over the years. Most of it had never reached the papers. There was just the occasional mention of a high-profile figure dying of unknown causes. Most of his hits were proactive, to keep a rising instigator from reaching his potential.

Putting the last file away, Jake found himself in a quandary. His employer expected him to take out Quint after he found out all he could about his present, past, and future assignments. But Jake was finding it hard to stay above the politics as usual. He prided himself on keeping his emotions out of his business, but Quint's records had made a very strong impression on him. In the past, he'd never thought about the right or wrong of things. It was just business— nothing personal. Now he had doubts about his own neutrality. He was not pleased with the way his mind was working. Keeping things simple had kept him out of trouble.

As he closed the file cabinet, the phone made an unpleasant noise, "Gun shop," he answered.

In the Name of Justice

It was the asshole who'd called him before. "We need to step up our operation. There is word out that your guy is going to make a very heavy hit in a few weeks. Your fee will be doubled with his termination. Don't forget, we need to know everything there is to know about him before you bring this to a satisfactory conclusion. Who he works for is of the highest importance."

The phone made a click. As Jake returned the receiver to its cradle, he was thinking he might be on the wrong side of the fence.

Checking into a motel for the night, Quint used the extra time to go over the file given to him by Hilda. From the first page he was intrigued by the magnitude of what he was expected to pull off. The three targets were not the usual suspects on their way up in the terrorist world. These guys were the main leaders in their respective parts of the world. When he took these three out, it would be headline news around the world and set the terrorists back years—something like cutting off the head of the snake.

The further he got into the file, the more ambitious it became. It seems his employers wanted to end the threat of high profile terrorism for years to come.

He was all for its lofty goals, but he couldn't possibly do this mission as a one-man operation. His apprentice would have to take a very active role.

80

Whenever he thought of Jake, he felt a little nudge, a twinge of something not on the level. The more he thought about it, the more he felt Jake was not the novice appeared to be. There was that self-assured presence about him that usually came from a well-trained, experienced, field-savy individual.

He would have to send Jake's prints to his friend at FBI headquarters to be sure who he was. Little nudges should be listened to every time. He would need real help on this job, and he didn't want to be looking over his shoulder. Putting the file aside, he called his connection, gave him Jake's background as he knew it, and told him the fingerprints would be on the way the following day. He would get Jake's prints from his concealed weapons permit, which was on file with his employment application.

Putting thoughts of Jake aside for the time being, Quint returned to the folder Hilda had given him. What she was requesting had all the makings of a worldwide headliner if he could pull it off. The three hits would change the makeup of all terrorist organizations and their sponsors.

Tyre, Lebanon, was a good place for a mini-summit. According to the information in the file, the leaders would arrive in the dark of night without the knowledge of the local government. The clandestine meeting was meant to resolve their differences. A leader would emerge from that meeting and bring all the world terrorists under one umbrella. That would be bad news for the free world. Constant bickering amongst the terrorists had kept the lid on their activities over the years. It was time to take them out and seal the lid. This operation should actually be done by the governments of the free world, but they had no stomach for the realities facing them. As usual, it would take the wit and wisdom of the private sector to do the dirty work for those who couldn't see past their political noses.

The file contained all the information Quint needed to take care of business. All he had to do was find his way to Tyre and set up his ambush. It would help if Jake turned out to be what he appeared. And maybe he could get Hilda out of the office and into the field.

The freeway north from Seattle was usually a mess, and this day was no exception. The traffic was anywhere from crawl to stop. Each off-ramp presented a problem that seemed not to have an issue once you passed it.

As Quint passed the Kingston Ferry off-ramp the cell vibrated, wanting his attention.

"Quint here."

There was a pause on the other end, which was not unusual with cell phones as one cell tower handed off to another along the highway. "Quint, I have news of your friend Jake. We don't need his prints for positive ID. You are right, he is not what he pretends to be. There is a file on him going back some five years. He's been a busy boy. There are at least ten unexplained deaths where he has appeared in one form or another. The reason he's still on the street is because most of the untimely deaths were people who probably deserved what they got, and it saved the FBI and the local and state governments huge amounts of money not having to chase down and prosecute the victims. There is a hands-off policy until he makes a big mistake. The guy has no conscience or loyalty as far as his file reads. He'll hire out to anyone if the money is right. So far he hasn't stepped on our toes. You best be careful; someone might not have your best interest at heart."

Before Quint could say thank you, the cell went dark. His friend was probably thinking that Jake wasn't doing anything more than Quint was doing.

Quint thought, *The difference between me and Jake is that for me the money is not the important thing, but taking out evil where I find it is.*

The only recourse he had was to test Jake.

It was near closing time for most of the shops on the long block where the gun store was located. The view from the shops was the array of fishing boats tied up in the harbor and the pleasure crafts floating peacefully at the private docks.

The open sign could be seen in the window as Quint pulled into the parking space designated for the gun store. The shop to the right was in the process of closing, and Jake could be seen through the bay window of the gun store talking with a customer.

With the file and his travel bag in hand, Quint locked the car, waved at the beauty salon on the left, and entered his shop.

Jake waved as Clint entered and the customer, having finished his business, left the store.

"How was the trip, Quint? I expected you earlier today," Jake said in an overly friendly tone. Quint saw that he was trying too hard to be the good employee, which meant he was feeling guilty about something.

As Quint put his things on the counter, he said, "Jake, close the shop, and we'll head for the back room. My employer has a job for me, and it's more than a one-man operation. I have the file folder in hand with the details. We'll go over it, and you can tell me what you think."

Quint had purposely spoken to Jake in a position of authority. He wanted to test how far he would grovel to keep his secret. Chances are he wouldn't abase himself very far.

Without saying a word, Jake began the procedure to close the store. The hair began to stand up on his neck at Quint's brusque attitude. Something was in the wind.

When the shop was properly put to bed, Jake walked around the counter and into the secret room in the back.

Quint was sitting at the large table where they assembled the exotic rifles and other weapons ordered for special operations worldwide. He'd laid out a large file folder at one end and was absorbed in the contents when Jake approached the table. "Have a seat, Jake, we have a lot to discuss," he said.

Jake, still wondering about Quint's stern manner, sat as he was asked.

Quint pushed three photos in front of Jake and inquired, "Do you recognize any of these guys?"

Jake spread the photos out and purposely took several minutes to view each one. Without looking up, he said, "If these guys are your new project, I would guess you have a death wish. I've read your files and even though you are very good at your line of work, it won't be easy to eliminate three heads of state! I don't believe something of this magnitude has ever been attempted."

Quint retrieved the pictures and remarked, "You can decide if you want to continue with your position here based on the fact you'll be an integral part of the operation. If you want out, now is the time to make the move. If you decide to stay on, we need to begin planning for the hits. Our first move will be a flight to Tyre. You don't have to make a decision this evening, but by the time we open the shop in the morning, I'll need a yea or nay. Go home and think it over; there will be no turning back."

Jake looked over at Quint. For the first time in his short but busy career, he had allowed a distraction from his tunnel vision, his determination to not let politics or emotion rule his thinking.

Quint's files had caused him to stop and think about his country and the people who wanted to destroy it. In the beginning he'd only wanted to use his skills with firearms. But he got caught up in the money. Leaving emotion out of his business, he'd overcome guilt. In his twisted logic, everyone was fair game. His only limit was children; anyone else was eligible for his sights. He figured the whole world was corrupt, and he was just thinning out the corruption. Why not get paid for doing the world a service? His loyalty was to himself alone.

In his two tours of duty in the Navy he'd been around the world plying his trade for chicken feed. Why not get paid some real money for doing the same thing on the outside?

The money consumed him. His character bent to fit the situation. His only thought was the next hundred thousand he would get for taking just one shot. The target mattered little; it was just that—a target. He saw only dollar signs when he pulled the trigger. He had no feelings or emotion for anything in his sights.

But after reading Quint's files, he discovered what that little voice was that tugged at him now and then: It was his conscience. He'd suppressed it in favor of money over the years, paying little attention to its yearning.

The files had opened his eyes to all the things he'd been taught in the Navy, all the things he'd let slip away. It was interesting how one could be so blinded by rapacity. Guilt had finally surfaced to push back the greed that had devoured him.

Jake brought himself back to the present and retorted, "I'll think on it this evening and have your answer in the morning."

He stood up and walked out of the secret room, wondering what the hell Quint was up to.

After Jake closed the front door, Quint finished up with the file. Any thoughts he had about Jake being an amateur were quelled. His reaction to the photos was a dead-bang giveaway. The guy was not a novice looking for a mentor.

What the FBI guy had said about someone not having his best interests at heart was right on. There was an old saying about keeping your friends close, and your enemies closer. Keeping Jake close would keep him honest.

Stringing Jake along until he could find out who had hired him would be tricky. It might be easier to just confront him and take him out, if push came to shove.

Putting the file away, Quint closed the secret door and walked around the counter and out the front door. He'd deal with Jake in the morning, but for now he needed some rest. The trip had been a quick turnaround, and sleep had not been the number one priority.

Jake spent the better part of the night trying to figure out how to explain his situation to Quint. He couldn't come up with anything that sounded like it would be successful. He didn't like this newfound conscience shit; not giving a damn about anything but himself had been so much easier.

He could see where thinking too much got a guy into trouble. Being one step ahead of everyone else was what kept men in his line of work alive. One mistake, and it was curtains.

It was near daylight when Jake decided to give up on the sleeping thing. He'd never had trouble sleeping before, and if this newfound conscience was the problem, it would be better to stay focused on money rather than people and country. The decision he was looking for wasn't happening, so playing along with Quint was the way to go.

Downing his third cup of coffee as he approached the gun store, Jake resolved to sit back and see how things panned out. He would stall his employer as long as possible. He had no intention of taking Quint out.

It would not be easy to disengage from his contract, having taken front money for the job. Usually anyone who wanted out was well on their way to the promised land before the payoff check arrived.

When he pulled into the designated parking spot in front of the gun store, his cell announced a call. "Jake here."

By the sound and tone of the voice on the other end, it was the same asshole who kept calling for him to speed things up. "We are becoming impatient with you, Jake. You need to take care of business soon. We've found out who your target works for, so that's not a problem. Take him down ASAP."

Jake shook the phone, wanting to put his hand through to the asshole on the other end and silence his irritating voice. "I'll take care of things at the first opportunity."

Jake closed the cell, ending the call.

He might have to use his hunting skills to break his contract, shooting them first to keep them off balance.

Putting the phone and the irritable caller aside, Jake opened the store for the day and waited for Quint to show up.

The last call had decided him: He would be truthful with Quint and join forces with him. He had been on the wrong side of the fence for too long. His country was more important than the money, and the evil he had to deal with was smothering him. He could see now that they had been leading him from lowlife targets in the beginning to higher-value targets, step by step. They were leading him up to something big time. Their intention was to get him buried so deep in their world, he'd not be able to back out.

He was shaken from his reverie by the bell clanging as Quint opened the front door and entered with his arms full of files, rolled-up maps, and a briefcase.

"Good morning, Jake."

Quint's tone was friendlier than the day before, so Jake figured he'd made some kind of decision about the job at hand.

Quint walked around the counter and let himself into the secret room. Jake followed. Quint laid everything on the assembly table, spreading out the maps and putting the file at the top of the maps to keep them from rolling up.

"If you're going with me, we need to get started with the planning. Have you decided what you want to do?" inquired Quint.

Jake put his hands on the bottom of the maps to hold them and said, "I'm in."

Quint retorted, "That sounds good, but there might be something you want to tell me before we begin here. Naturally I investigated your background when I hired you. My friend at the FBI sent me some interesting things about you. You seem to have left a lot out of your resume."

"Well, Quint, I suppose we can quit the pussyfooting around and lay it all on the table. You evidently know what I do and have done in the past. But there are some things you don't know.

"I was hired to take you down, after I found out who your employers were and what your next mission was. I intended to do just that—until I read your files. I had an awakening of sorts. Like a preacher would say, I've seen the light.

"I won't go into the details, but suffice it to say I'm on your team, thick or thin. I can prove myself, because the only way out for me from my employers is to take them out. They don't know that I know where they are and who they are. We only had contact by phone and drop points. But I discovered things by accident. They are in the same area as your project. We could make it a double feature and do the world a great service."

"Jake, you expect me to believe you can do a turnaround in your life's philosophy in the short time you've been working in my shop? You've been a cold-blooded killer, without regard for good or evil, with money your only motivation. You're telling me that deep inside somewhere there was a conscience just waiting for the opportune time to show itself?"

"Yes sir, that's exactly what I'm saying. I don't have a clue what happened, but it's real and I intend to use my skills in the same manner as you do. Let's put my past to bed and concentrate on killing the bad guys worldwide."

Quint looked into the blue eyes of Jake, trying to find a hint that his story was all bullshit The eyes, face, and body movements didn't signal deceit.

"Okay, Jake, let's do it this way. I'm betting you're on the square, but I still have reservations about your motives. The first sign I get that you are not being honest with me, I won't say anything: I will kill you, and not even think twice about it. You won't know when it's coming. If that makes you uncomfortable, then you better head out that door and call it a day."

Jake, with a smile on his face, retorted, "I don't have a problem with that. I only hope someone else doesn't make me look bad and pow, you follow through."

Chapter Seven

The Team

Hilda was trying to work her way into the field. She hated being cooped up in the maze of offices. She would only feel alive with hands-on participation in the clandestine operations that came across her desk. That brought up her old friend Quint. She was the control agent for his operation. If he wanted to take her along, she would have plenty of excuses for being in the field. Covering her ass wouldn't be a problem; staying alive might be. Quint's assignment in a volatile part of the Middle East was so dangerous that one spark from any direction could find the whole region in total anarchy, with free-fire zones measured in miles, not blocks.

With everything out in the open between them, Quint and Jake began in earnest to get the show on the road. They rolled the maps out again. On the first map Quint pointed out the buildings where their targets were reportedly meeting. The days and times were listed on the left ledger. The second map showed the layout of the meeting rooms. The whole building would be an armed camp. Its location near the waterfront was a plus for the targets, but also for themselves. The harbor would provide easy ingress and egress for the participants at the meeting. They could arrive by boat and not have to deal with any prying eyes watching the airports or border crossings. Even though the meeting was supposed to be secret, it would be hard to hide that many heads of state going to the restroom, let alone to a hotbed like Lebanon.

Tyre was a ancient seaport with many tales to tell and a sandy bottom scattered with new and old relics of the sea. With the busy port full of ships from all over the world plying their trade and the thousands of pleasure craft that anchored there annually, one could sail into it without much notice.

Quint remarked, "I was thinking we'd find our way to Alexandria, Egypt. From there we rent a sizeable cabin cruiser and sail to Port Said. We wouldn't be noticed any more than a thousand others.

"I know an arms smuggler in Port Said. It's on the way. We can load up the cruiser there, and no one will be the wiser. He can also fix us up with the proper maritime papers in the event we get checked out by the local coast guard."

In the middle of the planning session Quint's cell chimed. The familiar voice on the other end spoke in a singsong manner, trying to disguise her voice, but it was in vain. "Hello, Hilda. Checking up on us so soon?"

There was a long pause before Hilda responded, "Not checking up on you, but I have a suggestion for your assignment. I think you need someone who has hands-on experience in the Port of Tyre."

Quint knew instinctively what was coming. "And who might that be?"

"Okay, just tell me you want me to go with you, okay? Three are better than two. This mission will be a convoluted mess of the first order from the get-go. You could use my expertise in the field on this one."

"Hilda, what can you add to the mission that we don't already have?"

Without any hesitation, Hilda responded, "Well, I've been there recently and know the location of all the military, as well as the local police. I was there on a fact-finding mission for another project. I also know the dock area and where the meeting building is located. You may find me to be a valuable asset."

"You have a good argument for going along. What's the downside?"

There was another pause, then Hilda played her aces. "I can stop the funding for your adventure, or at least delay it. You know—make things difficult."

Quint put his hand over the receiver and said to Jake, "We'll be having a third party for our trip. Any objections to having a very good field agent go along? One who also happens to be an attractive female?"

"No problem, boss," Jake shot back.

"Hilda, get your ass up here pronto, like tomorrow, so you can sit down with us and get this thing ironed out. Time is not on our side."

Quint closed the cell. Just as they returned to the maps, Jake's cell buzzed. The connection was a bit fuzzy, but Jake could understand the meaning and harsh tone. "Jake, you have one week to complete this assignment. You know the penalty for failure." The asshole's voice was so annoying Jake closed the cell.

"Quint, I think my contact is losing his patience. He'll be threatening me with death on the next call. My first bullet will be between his eyes."

While they were checking out the maps and discussing their options, Quint remarked, "You know, I've been thinking about our appearance. Here we are heading for the Middle East, and you look like a California surfer dude. And I look more like a Midwest farmer than a Middle Eastern type. Then along comes Hilda, big girl, blond and blue. We'll stick out like a redwood tree in Death Valley. I believe we need to add a fourth member to the team. We can only wear so many disguises before we become suspicious.

"I have a friend who works in our world. He would fit right in with the local population. He's about five eleven, two-ten, black and hazel. The guy speaks several languages used in that part of the world. If he's not busy, maybe we can get him to join the team. With Jett on the team, we'll have someone who can roam the local area, listen to the street chatter, and recon our objectives.

"Jett Horn is a vet who's spent time with the Army Special Forces, Navy SEALs and the National Security Agency, as well as doing a tour with drug enforcement south of the border. He's a standout with the cabal that I work for. He's a man of few words and fewer friends. He lost a couple of buddies over the years and now he only works alone. We've crossed paths a few times on different assignments, and we got along well. Hilda would know where he is.

"I'll have a chat with him about our dilemma and ask for his assistance. He'll understand our predicament from his past experiences, and with a little luck he'll agree to give us a hand."

Quint opened the sliver of a phone and punched in Hilda's special number. The cell buzzed five times before Hilda's voice traveled over the several states between her location in New Mexico and Washington. "Hilda here."

"Hilda, Quint. I need to ask a favor for the benefit of the upcoming mission."

After a short pause, Hilda could be heard saying to someone, "Please wait outside."

"Sorry, Quint, I was in the middle of a strategy meeting. What can I do for us?"

"There's another operative who works like I do. His name is Jett Horn. He would be our best asset on the upcoming job. If you can locate him, I would like to ask him to go along. I suppose you have the ability to check out his file. After you screen his package, you'll understand how well he'll fit in with us."

"Okay, Quint, I have enough time to go through his profile before I catch a flight. I'll bring a way to contact him with me. See you later tomorrow. I'm going to catch the shuttle to Bellingham and rent a car. You won't need to worry about meeting me."

The cell went blank.

Quint was used to the cell going blank without any salutations. Hanging on to a conversation too long was not healthy. Everyone in the business seem to have similar habits.

"Jake, Hilda will be here tomorrow afternoon. She'll bring us a way to contact Jett. In the meantime we can do our planning with four operatives in mind. If he doesn't want in, we'll scale back. I suppose the first thing we need is a rental agent for the boat and quarters. Have you been in that part of the world?" Quint took his seat at the table full of maps.

Jake thought about his last adventure in the Middle East and answered, "I was in the area once, but not in Tyre. I took on a hit job for a gangster who wanted a rival gang member eliminated. It was easy money."

"Well, Hilda will have some insight on what's available since she's been there recently."

Hilda pulled the rental car into the parking space just down from the gun shop. There was a slight mist falling, which made the harbor and the outer bay seem to be in limbo. The boats were rocking gently from the tide coming in, giving the whole scene a Norman Rockwell look.

Hilda could understand why someone would want to live in this small city with its slow pace and easy access to downtown.

After locking the car she walked back to the gun store wondering if she had even needed to lock up. Looking through the store window, she could see a young man behind the counter showing a customer a handgun. Quint was not visible, but then he'd mentioned something about a back room where they worked on special orders.

When she opened the shop door, a bell announced a visitor; the young man behind the counter looked up, pushed a button next to the cash register, waved and said, "Hello, Hilda. Quint will be right out."

Quint appeared from the door behind the counter, smiled and said, "This way, Hilda."

Hilda found her way around the end of the counter, slipping behind the young man, who was now demonstrating the proper way to field strip a Colt .45, and she followed Quint through the door. He gestured to a seat at the table with all the maps strewn about. Smiling, he remarked, "Hilda what possessed you to finagle your way into the field?"

Hilda ignored the question, "I have a number for your friend Jett Horn. He hangs out on a ranch in Belize; it's only accessible by aircraft. He enjoys his privacy. Like you, with all the shit he's done, personal safety is a major accomplishment. Jett must have half the terrorist and gangster world wanting him dead. I'm surprised either of you is alive!"

Quint felt a twinge of uneasiness. There was something different in Hilda's demeanor. He had first noticed it at their meeting in New Mexico. She seemed detached, like a robot going through the motions—not knowing, just doing. Putting aside the little voice in the back of his head, he said, "You look great. The office job must agree with you, but then you're here. What's up?"

"The office job is boring, about as much fun as watching grass grow or paint dry. I don't feel alive." Changing the subject abruptly, Hilda continued, "Your guy Horn is at his ranch as we speak. He's in between jobs right now and could possibly be available—his choice. I hope you know what you're doing, he is one badass son of a bitch. From what I've heard he doesn't like anybody, any place, or any thing. According to his profile, he spends his off time diving, flying, and riding his motorcycle. He's a loner, with one exception: a very attractive blond is with him on occasion. No one knows anything about her. He keeps her out of his affairs. So what's with all the maps?"

Quint's little voice whispered to him again, and again he pushed it aside. "We're in the middle of getting our ducks lined up for the mission. Since you've been in Tyre recently, you might remember a place that we could rent to set up a safe house. Something near the waterfront in case we need to take a powder in a hurry."

Hilda responded, "Not a problem," as she handed Quint a paper with Jett's number on it.

Quint took the paper. "Hilda, you might look over the maps and pin the location for the secret summit meeting and where they'll be quartered for the visit. They won't have to worry about the rent, since their earthly concerns will be eliminated."

As Hilda turned her attention to the map-laden table, Quint stepped into the office at the rear of the room, where the shop had a secure phone. With most of the shop's business conducted on the dark side, it was essential to be able to speak freely, and a secure landline was the best option.

Quint dialed the number Hilda given him. After the fifth ring, a voice answered, *"Hola, buenos dias."*

Quint countered, *"¿Habla usted ingles?"*

The woman answered, *"Si, hablo un poco."*

Trying to remember his Spanish, Quint replied, "Jett Horn, *por favor.*" There was a long pause on the other end, with some loud but unintelligible conversation in the background. Finally, a man's voice came on the phone. "I don't recognize your phone number, and I don't know how you got mine, but because you've piqued my interest, what say you?"

Quint responded, "*¿Como esta?* This is Quint. Hilda gave me your number. She told me you were on vacation and didn't have much to do. So I thought I'd give you a call and see if you wanted to fill some of your free time with a little adventure. I have a project in the works that would be right up your alley. I'm surprised they didn't offer you this project before contacting me. There will be four of us if you decide to come along. It involves three—maybe four—high-ranking international leaders who are becoming a problem for the free world.

"The good guys are paralyzed and can't do anything about the surge of these leaders who want to destroy western civilization and the free enterprise system and bring the world back to the Dark Ages. The western populace doesn't understand what's going on, so our bosses have decided to cut the head off the snake. We can do the job without all the strings attached to formal governments. What do you think? *Es urgente.*"

The phone was silent for a brief moment before Jett responded. "Quint, in those few words, you've just asked me to help you turn the whole world upside down! Change the course of history and help millions of people sleep through the night. Have you gone bonkers? I'm sure I know the leaders you're talking about, and the task sounds like a pipe dream. I'll need a lot more information before I agree to a suicide mission like you're proposing."

"Jett, fly up here to Washington. Hilda and I will explain the details. I know you usually work alone, but this is a project unsurpassed in its daring. It will relieve governments far and wide, and since we'll do it right, no one will know who did the world a favor. Once again, our people will not get the applause they deserve. We, like our government special ops brothers, go about our business with little or no recognition, and none is expected. A job well done in our circles means we are the only ones who know."

"Okay, Quint, you've got my interest."

Chapter Eight

Details

The flight from Belize to Bellingham, Washington was uneventful, which was always a good sign when one challenged Mother Nature. Jett had always been better at landings than takeoffs, so the small airport was not a problem; it resembled his own airstrip.

Jett parked the plane in extended parking, rented a car, and made his way up to Blaine. Following the directions Quint had given him, he parked his car across the street from the gun store. As he locked the car, the view of the tranquil harbor caught his eye. A few fishing boats were heading out into Puget Sound to ply their trade. Pleasure craft outnumbered the commercial boats, which were giving way to the influx of upscale yuppies from the Seattle area trying to find a quiet, less-traveled community. Blaine was close enough to get away for the weekend and leave the congested urban area behind. Forty-eight hours out of the rat race would clear the head and settle the nerves.

Using the crosswalk, Jett made his way across the old highway that doubled as Blaine's main street, once the only way to travel from Seattle to Vancouver, Canada.

Making his way over to the gun store, Jett entered, triggering the bell that announced a customer.

Hilda, Quint, and Jake were standing at the end of the counter drinking coffee. Quint held out his hand to Jett as he approached the counter. After a short handshake, Quint said, "Jett, may I introduce Hilda? I'm sure you've dealt with her over the phone. And this is Jake, a young fellow who has made his mark in our world."

"Yes, hello Hilda! You are surely the most attractive handler that I've ever had the pleasure to meet. Jake, I haven't heard of your exploits, but if Quint thinks highly of you, I will follow his lead. Now, not to waste any time, let's get on with convincing me to join your happy little group!"

Quint lifted the counter top for Jett to join them behind the display case. With Jake leading the way, the group made their way into the back room. The video monitors placed around the interior and exterior of the store would give them a heads-up when a customer was about to enter.

Quint suggested they gather around the map table to put the magnitude of the mission in perspective.

"Jett, the Axis of evil will be meeting in Tyre in a couple of weeks. We intend to eliminate the Axis, along with all their first lieutenants. The method is still up in the air. We were waiting to run it by you. There are a multitude of options here, and we have unlimited funds to accomplish the mission."

Jett pondered the maps, then queried Hilda. "Ninety percent of the time our employers have the correct information. How sure are you about this one? The ten percent that is usually out there bothers the shit out of me!"

Hilda looked a little taken aback by the question. She tried to look calm as she responded, "I have had control of this mission from the get-go. There is no percentage of wrong information here. This affair is tight."

Jett shot back, "I don't suppose you want to share with us your source for such reliable information?"

"That information is not open for discussion, Jett, you know that. Why do you ask?" Hilda almost shouted. Her calm manner was dissolving rapidly.

"Lighten up, Hilda. I'm not questioning your leadership with the company, but then again, I don't know how much field experience you have. I don't want any surprises when we get to Tyre."

Quint stepped in. "I've been in the field with Hilda—she'll do just fine."

The little voice was jerking at Quint again, but he couldn't figure out what the hell was bothering him. Putting it aside, he added, "We made a daring escape from a hot spot in Central America some time back, and Hilda performed like an old pro."

Jett seemed to soften a little with Quint vouching for Hilda in a real-world situation. "Okay, Quint, I'll go with your evaluation of Hilda under fire. Hilda, as you well know, people in our business can't have any loose ends or doubts about the company they keep. I'm sure you would be as critical of someone you didn't know as I am. Now that we're all on the same page, let's get down to business."

Hilda threw out the first suggestion. "I was in Tyre recently, but I wasn't aware of this mission at the time, so I didn't pay any particular attention to the area where we need to go. It might be a good idea for me to return and check out the best spot for a safe house. I won't draw too much attention, since I was just there, and they're used to seeing me.

Jett looked across the table. His eyebrows wrinkled towards his nose. "I believe you contacted me because I can roam the streets of any Middle Eastern city without notice. I fit the profile, and I speak most the dialects in the area. If this is the case, the logical person to head for Tyre and get things going is me."

Quint looked over at Hilda for a rebuttal, and she remarked, "I can't argue with that logic. I think you should be the advance party for this mission."

Quint said, "Okay, with that out of the way, the next question that comes to mind is weapons. Jett, do you know an arms dealer we can trust to get us what we need for the mission?"

Jett shot back, "Yes, I do know a guy who can help us. He is an Irishman of Jewish descent. He simply calls himself the Jew. The guy is a bit long in the tooth, having fought in every war since the early forties. He's only sixty-five inches tall, one hundred forty pounds, white and blue. The white mop is his trademark, and the only reason he's still alive is because he deals with all sides. He says there are going to be two more Middle East wars, and he's up to the challenge to fight in both. He has the resources to supply us with anything from automatic rifles to tanks. I believe the only thing he can't get is a suitcase nuke. I'll contact him the minute I step off the plane."

Jake looked up from the maps and suggested, "After studying the maps, I believe we should charter a plane and fly into Cyprus as a team. In Cyprus we can lease a decent-size cabin cruiser and sail over to Tyre. We can anchor there and not have to deal with all the border shit. We'll have easy access to the waterfront where the Axis have their meeting place planned. And in the event we have to make a hasty departure, the boat will serve us well. With the chartered plane and boat, we can avoid the strict customs inspections and bring some of our more exotic small weapons along."

The table grew very quiet as they all thought about what Jake had suggested. Then Hilda spoke up. "I can call my office and have them charter us a plane and check on finding a boat that will meet our needs."

Quint responded, "Sounds good to me. What do you think, Jett?"

Jett didn't respond quickly, but instead reached for the pointer and addressed the map. "Well, if we can put a boat right here in the harbor, we'll be able to go ashore and return with little notice. The harbor is crowded at this point with pleasure craft from around the world. We'd just be one more group of tourists in the Mediterranean looking to discover some ancient underwater relics. Yes, I think Jake has hit it right on the head. Good thinking, Jake!"

Quint said, "Its getting late. Let's call it a night."

Hilda returned to her motel room and punched in the confidential number on her cell. It rang four times before Rita picked up.

"Yes, Hilda," came Rita's voice from the other end.

"Rita, I need a charter plane large enough for a transatlantic flight at Sea-Tac by the day after tomorrow. And along with that, call Larnaca, Cyprus and arrange for a large cabin cruiser for two weeks. Call me with the details when you're finished."

Quint and Jett left the gun shop for Jake to close up and headed down the street to the coffee shop for a late snack. The place was not crowded so they had a corner booth without any ears nearby.

The waitress looked to be near fifty and had put on a lot of miles over the years, but she was pleasant enough for someone working the graveyard shift.

After the coffee was delivered, Jett remarked, "I get bad vibes from your friend Hilda. I don't believe she is as advertised. You know that little tug you get when something isn't what it appears to be? Well, I'm getting more than a little tug."

"You know, Jett, now that you've brought it up, I've been getting that same nudge from out of the blue when she's around. I don't know where it comes from, because she proved herself in the past. Of course, it has been some years since our adventure in Central America. I think we should keep close tabs on her and look for anything that might prove her to be something more than the persona she's presenting to us.

"Hilda has worked for the cabal nearly as long as I have. With the extensive background investigation they do, it would be hard for her to have a secret past or present. But it's always prudent to listen to your inner voice."

When the pie and coffee were nearly finished, the weathered waitress passed by the table to drop off the check and remarked, "Tonight, along with serving, I'm the cashier, cook, and dishwasher. If you feel a little tipsy it wouldn't hurt my feelings."

She shuffled off, heading for the counter where the antique cash register was located.

Quint picked up the check and said, "Let's hang it up for tonight. In the morning I'll get in touch with a friend at the cabal headquarters and run a double check on Hilda. My friend would know about dirt on anyone. He works in personnel."

Jett nodded. He looked tired—it had been a long day. "How about breakfast at ten and then back to planning?"

They shook hands and left the all-night diner.

Quint returned to the house he'd bought years before but seldom had the opportunity to enjoy. Picking up the landline, he called the cabal headquarters and left a message for his friend to check out Hilda's history from day one, asking additionally for his opinion of her past and present job performance.

Jett's vibes were nearly the same as his own, so there must be something to the Hilda thing. He'd know in the morning if anything was off-color with her tenure.

The following morning Quint's landline announced a caller, and he picked up the receiver on the second ring. "Quint here."

The familiar voice on the other end reported, "As to Hilda, her file has been flagged, but with a low priority watch. Seems she has some political views not in keeping with the cabal's. She has gone from capitalism, to socialism and communism, and then to Islam. Who knows what she may decide to do next? But she does excellent work, so some things are overlooked. Everyone who works here has a past. Hers is no more of less intriguing than many others.

112

"That said, there is a note at the bottom of her file jacket that says, *Update this file every two months.* I would be vigilant. I'll keep my eyes open, and if anything comes up, you'll be the first to know."

Quint returned the receiver to its cradle. He wondered if Hilda had turned against the West completely. She'd certainly enjoyed the benefits of the West with her political actions in Central America. If she was working both sides of the fence, who the hell was running her?

Jake entered the shop at the usual opening hour, but only to put a sign in the window that the shop would be open for business at eleven. Then he headed down to the cafe to join Jett and Quint for breakfast.

He'd had a bad night. His handlers had been very rude with their threats to have him put on a hit list if he didn't make sure Quint was planted in the local cemetery. He was trying to put them off until he got to Lebanon, but they were like pit bulls. His only way out of the contract was to kill his employer, and killing that piece of work would be a pleasure.

Leaving the shop, he found his way to the cafe and took a seat with the two purveyors of death to evildoers around the world, striking where governments and legalities would have overshadowed the crime, allowing international criminals to go free and never pay for their deeds. Their employers were not bound up with a convoluted, mind-numbing set of outdated legal procedures designed to favor the accused, relying on the worthy concept that it was better to allow ten guilty to go free rather than mistakenly prosecute one innocent person. But that was before terrorism and suicide bombers had become a worldwide phenomenon.

As he approached the table, he could hear Jett telling Quint, "I know a way to stop all the suicide bombings around the world. It would not be something for the faint of heart to undertake. It would be a job for someone with ice water in their veins."

"How the hell are you going to stop all the suicide bombers around the world?" asked Jake as he took a seat in the booth.

Quint chimed in, "Yeah, what would you have to offer them that's better than a paradise full of young virgins?"

Jett smiled and said, "Not a big deal with the DNA testing we have today. Look at it this way. When a suicide bomber blows himself up, he takes as many with him as possible—the more the merrier. Right?

"The bomber wins every time, because he doesn't suffer a penalty for his deed. His death is rewarded in the afterlife—in his mind. Well, with DNA, the suicide bomber can be identified. Once there is positive ID, you send a hit man to take out the bomber's father, mother, brothers, and sisters. The bomber killed someone else's mother, father, sister, or brother. Why should his family be free and guiltless, praising him for becoming a martyr, condoning the killing of other people's mothers and fathers?

"Once the word gets out what would happen to any suicide bomber's immediate family, there would be second thoughts about killing yourself to kill others, for one cause or another. Once you know your parents and others will be following you to paradise, the suicide bombings will slow to a trickle."

"Jesus, Jett, do you have any idea how cruel that sounds? What if the parents didn't praise the bomber for his deed?" asked Quint.

"Doesn't matter whether the parents are proud or not. The only way to stop terrorism is to *terrorize the terrorist*.

"There's one more aspect to this way of dealing with terrorism: all those who enable these people need to feel the sting of reprisal from somewhere. That's where the cabal comes in. We are willing to stretch the limits of the legal system, the limits of social conscience, and cross the void between what is right, versus what is presumed to be right. Evil is evil no matter where you find it. Anyone or any group who determines that others should die because they don't believe as they do is evil and should be dealt with accordingly."

Jake nodded at Jett and said, "I agree. The suicide bomber has to know there are consequences for his final act on earth. He's not going to get away with killing himself and taking as many others with him as possible without some kind of penalty.

"If the family knows they'll pay for the suicide bomber's deed, they won't be so anxious to push him towards martyrdom. And they certainly won't produce any more to take his place."

As the three were ordering breakfast, Hilda came through the door. She waved at their table and came over. "I have news about our air transport, and I have a seagoing vessel for us when we arrive at our destination."

Quint stood and motioned Hilda to have a seat, while the waitress poured her coffee and warmed up the others.

"Would you like something to go along with your coffee?" the waitress inquired of Hilda.

"Just a sweet roll, please."

They chatted about the town, the bay, and the invasion from Seattle while downing their breakfast.

It was a short walk to the gun shop after breakfast, and when they arrived a few customers were standing around wondering why the store hadn't opened yet. Quint unlocked the door, and they filed in. Hilda and Jett walked around the counter into the back room, while Quint and Jake waited on the potential buyers.

It didn't take long for the customers to do their business, and with the cameras doing their job, Quint and Jake joined Hilda and Jett at the map-strewn table.

When the quorum had assembled, Hilda stood and announced, "I can report this morning that our charter plane will be at Sea-Tac ready to depart at our pleasure tomorrow morning. And we have secured a forty-foot-plus Nordic Tug for two weeks. The tug is more than adequate for our lodging and transportation needs. It's also large enough for an open ocean sail if we need it. We can go right from Larnaca International Airport to the waterfront without much interference from the local authorities. But we need to stay out of northern Cyprus; it's controlled by the Muslims."

Jake, not being from the coast, was puzzled. Why on earth would anyone want to hire a tugboat for their mission? So, he asked, "Why would we want a tugboat?"

Hilda answered, "Its not really a tug; Nordic Tug is the style of the boat. It has similar lines as a tug, hence the name. This tug is passenger friendly in all aspects. We were lucky to find her on such short notice."

"Good work, Hilda. We can finalize our plans once we're on the ground in Tyre and collect some real-time intelligence," responded Quint.

In the Name of Justice

Chapter Nine

Port of Tyre

Quint put *Closed for Vacation* signs in the bay window and on the door. It would be at least two weeks before their return—assuming everything went according to Hoyle. With the two rental vehicles loaded, the four-member team headed for Sea-Tac, where their charter flight would be warmed up and ready for the long journey to Cyprus.

Leaving Blaine behind, Quint looked in the rearview mirror, which had become an all-too-often event, and watched the small town disappear. One day the mirror would be put away, and his daily view would be from the bow of a nice cabin cruiser.

After a two-hour ordeal with the traffic, they arrived at the airport to find the plane on the tarmac ready for takeoff. With special permission from the Transportation Security Administration, they drove the vehicles out to the plane and loaded their gear, then returned the cars to the rental agency and took off.

The view was breathtaking as the pilot made the final approach to Larnaca on Cyprus, the largest island in the Eastern Mediterranean. The intensely blue-green water surrounding the dozens of smaller islands seemed to glow with an inner light.

The landing was smooth. The weather had been their friend for the whole journey. Quint looked out the small window. "What a beautiful sight. Too bad the inhabitants can't find some common ground to enjoy the beauty."

Jett nudged Quint. "I have that tugging again. The hair on my neck is beginning to bristle. I can't put my finger on its origin, but it's as real as it gets."

Quint looked out the porthole-sized window again, and responded, "Those same little voices have been tugging at me since we left the friendly skies of the United States."

Hilda yelled out from the cockpit, where she had been watching the landing, "Our transportation is waiting. We'll be on our way to the waterfront and the Nordic Tug within the hour. Soon as we park, the customs people will make a cursory inspection of the plane and baggage. I made arrangements for them to rubber stamp our short stopover. The plane will fly on to Beirut and wait for us there in case there's a change in plans."

Jake had been looking out the port window. He kept thinking the airport should be on the starboard, but the tarmac they landed on was on the port. Something was up in River City. He moved to the seat next to Quint and said, "This is not Larnaca International. We are in the northern part of Cyprus. It is controlled by the Muslims—probably not our friends. Hilda must know what the hell is going on."

Quint jumped up and made his way to the cockpit, yelling over the noise of the engines as they taxied to their parking place, "Turn the plane around and take off. Do it now!"

Hilda, standing between the pilots, pulled a pistol out and aimed it at the pilot. "Shut the engines down now."

Just as Hilda finished her threat to the pilots, Jake, using the only weapon he had on his person, sent a dart from his handheld blowgun into Hilda's right temple. It was just a dart with nothing sinister on the tip. The dart distracted Hilda long enough for Quint to take the pistol down and pin Hilda to the back of the pilot's seat.

As he pulled the pistol from Hilda's hand, Quint shouted at her, "What the fuck are you doing?"

Even using all her strength, Hilda couldn't get free of Quint's hold. She yelled back, "Do you think for one minute I bought all that capitalist bullshit and the part about Jesus returning to save the world? Mohammed and Islam are the truth and the way. You can rest assured that your days are numbered. This plane will never get off the runway."

Those were her last words before Jett grabbed her throat and held it long enough for her to pass out. He then suggested, "Don't turn the plane around, Quint.

We can go along with the program and find out who else is involved in this scheme. I'm sure the tug is where they plan to take us down. Since we have been forewarned, we can rid this part of the world of a few more bad guys. At least we know for sure where the goose bumps have been coming from."

Jake and Jett put Hilda in the first passenger seat behind the cockpit, while Quint told the pilots to continue as they had been instructed by Hilda. They were both a little shaky, not knowing what the hell was going on.

The copilot said in a high-pitched voice, "She didn't give us any special instructions. We were told to land the plane in Paphos, then fly to Beirut, and hang there until further notice."

As the copilot was talking, the pilot parked the plane in the designated parking area and shut down the engines.

There was a van and an SUV to take them and their gear to the docks where the tug was located. Both vehicles pulled up to the plane, and two guys from each vehicle jumped out to help.

Looking out the cockpit window, Jett remarked, "Shit, we have company."

Jake was sitting with Hilda, holding her up in case the guys on the ground were looking to see if she was in the plane. He said, "I suppose we can claim she has airsickness and load her into the SUV. They'll have to go along with the program already laid out, so as not to arouse our suspicions."

As the pilot opened the hatch and they began to deplane, the ground crew and customs were busy retrieving, checking, and transferring their gear to the van. Jett stopped the ground crew and said they'd take care of things and to get on with whatever was necessary to get the plane ready for its return trip. The customs guy took a powder along with the ground crew.

Jett asked the driver to turn the van around and back it up to the plane. While he was doing that he separated the bag with their handguns from the others and walked it over to the SUV. He threw the bag into the rear seat like it was just a bag with their personal kits in it. The driver and his shotgun rider could have worked for a New York cab company. Their profile was perfect, with one exception: they were surely on the team to terminate the three gringos.

Jett pretended he didn't understand the language as the four conversed, thinking they would not be understood. He asked in English, "How far to the boat? Hilda has airsickness and shouldn't travel too far. She just needs some rest to get back on her feet."

The ugliest of the four answered in broken English, "It is less than fifteen minutes to the docks."

Jett responded, "We'll bring Hilda down from the plane and put her in the SUV. If she doesn't respond after we get to the boat, is there a doctor in the neighborhood?"

The ugly one looked at his friends questioningly, and they just shrugged their shoulders, so he answered,

"Yes, there is one not far from the docks. Would you like to stop on the way down?"

Jett replied, "No, I'm sure she'll be fine with a little rest, but thanks for offering."

The four huddled up near the rear of the van after it was loaded. Jett could read their lips from the short distance.

Mr. Ugly was saying to his friends, *"What do we do now? The woman was supposed to give the signal to the ambush team. We were to take the bodies to the boat and drop them in the middle of the crossing over to Lebanon."* The shortest of the four said, *"We take the route planned, and when we see the ambush team, we give the signal. If she dies in the process, it was Allah's will."*

Jett relayed the conversation to Jake and Quint, suggesting they look out for a good ambush spot and be ready to take the four out when the shooting started.

Quint said, "Jake, you ride in the van and shoot those two fuckers when the shit hits the fan. We'll take down the two in the SUV. Hopefully, we'll have a chance to do some damage to those who lie in wait. We won't have any problem finding the boat. I'm sure there aren't many Nordic Tugs in this part of the world. If we have a problem, Hilda will have come to by then and can give us what we need to know."

Quint and Jett carried Hilda from the plane to the SUV and strapped her into the third row of seats. They sat in the second row behind the front buckets.

124

The driver put his hand out the window and waved for the van to follow. They took off with tires screeching on the tarmac, heading for the coast.

Leaving the airport proper, the two-vehicle caravan turned onto a double-wide street that wound its way through some crowded parts of Paphos and towards the fishing harbor.

Hilda was beginning to moan in the back, so Jett put her out once again, while the two dumbfucks in the front jabbered away, still thinking they couldn't be understood.

Jett whispered, "The driver thinks something is wrong with the whole plan they laid out. He wants to call his friends to explain about Hilda, but the other one thinks they need to let things alone, lest the others think them to be cowards."

The road had narrowed to a two-lane, and there was little traffic. Soon the Mediterranean came into view. Many condos and homes were crowded along the hillsides overlooking the harbor.

"I think they'll make their move on the boat, maybe after we put to sea. It's a little crowded to be having an ambush in plain daylight with so many eyes. How are you sailor skills, Jett?" asked Quint.

The caravan slowed as the road began to wind its way to the beach. Looking back, Quint couldn't see the van. He asked the driver where the van was. The driver looked in his rearview mirror and remarked, "I don't see him."

Jett told the driver to pull over and call the van to find out where they were.

The hook-nosed driver came to a bend in the road and used the extra-wide part of the turn to get the SUV off the pavement. Even then, there was not near enough room for anyone to pass the vehicle without paying close attention. The road had been built hundreds of years ago and, except for the pavement, had not been improved much.

When they had come to a complete stop, Hook Nose tried to call the van. After two attempts he said, "He no answer. We no can turn around here, but down the road a ways is a turnout, and we can go back and check."

Quint responded, "Head down the road and turn around. Be quick about it!"

Hook Nose was having trouble deciding if he should continue or just wait for a signal from the van, and his partner was jabbering, *"We need to act! Something has gone wrong. Pull the pin!"*

Jett, understanding every word, yelled, "Quint, take the driver down," as he pulled his .45 and shot the guy riding shotgun in the back of the head.

Hook Nose was trying to get his shirt open to pull the pin on his waist belt loaded with TNT, but before he could find the pin, Quint broke his arm with the butt of his pistol. He wanted to keep the lowlife alive to find out what the hell they had planned.

While Quint was busy trying to disable the explosive belt, Jett punched in Jake's number. No response. He yelled, "Quint, let's tie and gag this asshole and get back up the mountain and check on Jake. He's not answering his cell. From what Hook Nose said, there has been a fuckup in their plans."

Quint pushed the dead man out the door, and he rolled down the mountainside, landing on a wide ledge not far from the road. He then walked the driver around and put him in the seat just vacated. Jett cut the safety belt loose from the rear seat and lashed the would-be suicide bomber tightly to the bucket seat and door, along with a gag in his runny mouth. He was still conscious, but in a lot of pain from his broken arm. Not being gentle, Jett grabbed his broken arm and asked, "Where are the others waiting?"

Hook Nose passed out.

Quint jumped into the driver's side and brought the SUV out onto the road and down the mountain looking for the turnout. A car came up behind them honking to pass. Quint, not knowing who was in the car, steered the SUV into the middle of the road, blocking the car. As they came to the turnout, he stopped just before it widened and jumped out with his pistol at the ready. The car behind them slammed on its brakes and screeched to a halt just inches from the rear of the SUV.

A young woman jumped out with her hands in the air, yelling, *"There's a van and two cars back up the mountain. One car is in front of the van the other to its rear. There are bodies lying all over the place. I just barely got by the mess. Could you help?"*

Quint didn't have a clue what the woman had said, but Jett translated her excited words, adding, "I don't know whether to trust what she's saying or not. She could be part of the ambush. I'll tell her to get the hell down the mountain and call the local authorities."

The woman apparently understood what Jett had just said to Quint for she returned to her car and waved for them to get out of the way. When Quint moved the SUV from the middle of the road, she sped past it with tires screeching.

Jett jumped into the back seat as Quint turned the SUV around, and they headed back up the mountain, hoping they were not too late to help Jake.

Quint said, "He can't be too far from where we turned around."

Jett was about to answer Quint when his cell vibrated. He retrieved the phone from the side cargo pocket on his trousers. "Jett here."

Over the gunfire in the background, Jake reported his situation. "I'm hit in the leg and there are bad guys on both sides of the road. I have a vehicle in front of me and one behind. I killed the driver and his partner. The partner had a TNT vest around his waist, but it either malfunctioned or I shot him before he could set it off. When you get here try not to hit him with something that might finish his attempt. The guys on the lower side of the road I can keep down, but the guys above me are the problem. If you stop at the bend just

128

before where we are, you can climb up and catch them by surprise."

His voice faded and the cell went blank.

Jett relayed the information to Quint and he slowed down, not wanting to come around a switchback and find themselves in the middle of a crossfire. Before each curve, they slowed down and listened for gunfire. On the third curve they could hear the battle.

Quint said, "I'll pull over and climb up the side here. I can get a shot at the bad guys from above. You keep an eye on Hilda and our friend here. I'll call when it's clear to drive around."

Quint was up the mountain and near the apex in no time. He could hear the rounds going off clearly as he peeked over the edge. Down below, the three vehicles were sitting on the side of the road, making the road nearly impassable.

He could see where the shots were coming from and wished he had his modified Remington 700 rifle to pick off the ambush team. Now he'd have to sneak up behind the two that he could identify and take them out.

Working his way down the craggy slope, he was upon the first shooter in less than five minutes. With the stealth of a mountain lion, he dealt him a fatal blow across the temple and now had a rifle to dispose of shooter number two.

Setting his sights on the puff of smoke coming from behind a rock some two hundred yards to his right,

129

Quint pulled the trigger on the rifle, and the round found its target. The hit was just below the ear on the man's left side. The scope was ancient but worked well. Taking the rifle and some papers he had found on the body, he headed over to search and recover anything of value from the second shooter.

Stopping to call Jett, he said, "Two down, two to go. The other two are over the bank, looking up at the van. Jake has them hunkered down, so it's okay to come up. We'll close from either side; it won't take much to do them in. I can see four bodies lying on the roadside. Jake must have had a fierce firefight. He's seen me now and waved for me to come down. See you when you come around the corner."

When Quint got to the van, Jake refused any help with his wounds, saying, "Take out those two fuckers down there first."

Jett pulled up in the SUV just as Quint was coming around the van to take a shot at the two left from the ambush team. He parked behind the car at the rear of the van and after checking on his prisoner and Hilda, he exited the front seat to join Quint.

"Jake said they were down to our right behind those two huge boulders there," Quint pointed out to Jett.

Jett responded as he moved off the road, "I'll crawl down and draw their fire, so you can pop them."

Quint nodded as Jett disappeared over the edge of the road, and he moved to the front of the car parked ahead of the van. From there he had a good view of the two boulders. He could see a rifle barrel sticking up between the two rocks, but couldn't get a decent shot. As he waited for Jett to draw fire, one of the terrorists darted out from behind the boulder and reached cover at the edge of the road.

Quint couldn't get a shot off at him, but when Jett jumped up near the boulders, the second guy left enough of his head showing to make an easy target for one quick shot. Most of the terrorist's head was gone before he hit the ground.

Quint turned just in time to see the SUV go up in a huge ball of fire. The explosion knocked him down and out.

Jett, who was behind the boulder checking out the dead body for papers and weapons, didn't get the brunt of the explosion. The van was moved nearly twenty feet, along with the vehicle in front of it. Jake tumbled out of the van as it began to roll towards the edge of the road. He cleared himself just as the van rolled over the edge and down the mountainside, plowing into the boulders where Jett was lying trying to clear his head from the terrific explosion that had his ears ringing so bad that he couldn't hear Jake yelling at him to stay put.

The van bounced off the boulders, and its momentum carried it on down the to the next switchback, where it landed in the middle of the road blocking any traffic coming up from the coast.

Jake, gunshot wounds in his leg and left shoulder, dragged Quint further away from what was left of the SUV, over across the road and next to the rock wall.

Jett crawled back up to the road and yelled out to Jake, "What the fuck happened? Jesus! You're bleeding all over the place. Is Quint still with us?"

Jake pulled Quint up to a sitting position, hoping to clear his head, and yelled back to Jett, "The wounded fucker evidently found the suicide belt in the SUV and triggered it. Quint is just knocked out. I don't see any visible wounds."

Jett made his way through the debris over to Jake, who said, "You don't look so hot either. You have blood running out of your ears."

Jett responded, "Damn, that was one hell of an explosion. I've not been that close to one in many moons. I can barely hear you, but it helps to know how to read lips."

They huddled over Quint, trying to arouse him and didn't notice the traffic backing up around the curve and the arrival of the police.

The police officer who seemed to be in charge said there were emergency vehicles on the way, but it would take some time to clear the van from the road to allow them to pass, because their emergency vehicles were coming up from the harbor.

Jett, not seeing a police car asked, *"How the hell did you get here?"*

The cop looked confused but then said, *"Motorcycle."*

Jake was feeling weak from shock and loss of blood, and couldn't understand any of the conversation. He hoped they were not in trouble with the local authorities.

Before the road below could be cleared, an ambulance arrived from Paphos. They began to attend to Jake, and with smelling salts, they brought Quint around. He opened his eyes and asked, "Did anyone in the van survive the blast?"

Jett, whose hearing was returning, replied, "We don't know. It's a real mess. I don't see how Hilda or the two bad guys could have made it."

The police officer turned the questioning over to the military officer who had just entered the first-aid station in the fishing harbor city of Kato Pafos.

The military officer spoke near perfect English as he addressed the trio of Americans. "As far as we can determine, you were attacked by terrorists at random. We have had trouble the past few months with some radical Islamists. Your credentials proved to be correct, and we're sorry you were caught in the middle of such a horrendous event. With that said, there are a couple of things that have troubled me, which were discovered during the investigation of the site."

"The bodies we found up on the mountain were shot in the head from the side. The body found below the edge of the road was also shot from the side. Someone was very accurate with a rifle and with the handgun shooting of the attackers in and around the explosion site. Do you have any explanation for this?"

Quint spoke up. "Yes sir. As you might guess, we are all retired American military. We were simply using our military skills to protect ourselves from attack. The attackers were not very skilled, except in blowing themselves up. They were vulnerable against any well-trained individuals. Their timing was bad. They simply picked the wrong target to make their statement."

Jett added, "We'd like to continue our journey. Would you be so kind as to provide us with transportation down to the Nordic Tug that is waiting for us? We are going to cruise the Mediterranean, stopping in Lebanon, and then going on to Gibraltar. We can heal our wounds on the trip."

The officer was not happy with the response, but didn't have any evidence to justify holding the trio any longer, so he suggested, "Gentlemen, I'm not happy about the incident or with your explanations. My sergeant will provide you with a ride down to the beach and your boat. I suggest you not return to this island again. We have pictures of you and will arrest you on sight. I'll think of something to hold you on at that time. My investigation will continue."

He turned and left the aid station. The sergeant pointed to a van outside the station. The trio loaded themselves into the van and were on their way to the tug.

The water was calm when the trio arrived at the small dock where the tug was moored. The sergeant dropped them off. He didn't bother to say adios, but just left them standing at the end of the dock.

Jett remarked, "They did a lot of talking, not knowing I could understand their tongue, and I surmise that they would love to find something to hold us on. The military officer will be doing his best to find something before we can cast off. I suggest we put to sea as soon as possible."

Quint said, "Jake you take the helm and get this thing fired up, while Jett and I go from stem to stern and check out what we have here. Hilda said the boat would be loaded with provisions for a two week cruise. We are now without any weapons, and I don't know if she had any put aboard or not. Soon as we finish our inspection we should get the hell out of here."

After a half-hour inspection, Quint declared the boat fit for the cruise. He hopped onto the dock and released the stern line while Jett let go of the bow line. As they climbed aboard, Jake pushed the throttle forward and the tug pulled away from the dock, heading into the Mediterranean. They were on their way to the port of Tyre and an uncertain destiny with some world class terrorists.

With the tug on autopilot, the trio had a meeting of the minds.

"We don't know for sure what happened to Hilda and the wounded bad guys. Common sense says they died in the explosion. The military guy didn't reveal if there was enough left to identify anyone or if they even found a body, let alone a woman. It was a good thing not to mention her, for it could have complicated things. The little nudges I get when there is trouble on the horizon say beware of the unknown," said Quint, the first to speak.

Jake was sitting in the captain's chair, his bandages beginning to show red. He'd moved around too much after the emergency room tech pulled the bullet out of shoulder and plugged the hole in his leg, where the bullet had gone clean through the fleshy part of the thigh. He said, "Unless Hilda got out before the idiot blew the van up, she couldn't have survived the explosion. I don't see how that was possible. She was groggy and tied up. It really sucks to have loose ends out there with no way to fix them. I suppose we're lucky to be sitting here talking."

Jett looked over at Jake and remarked, "You look like an ad for a safety magazine on how not to do something.

"On the off chance that Hilda somehow got out of the van and disappeared on us, it would be prudent to dump this tug and find something she doesn't know about. As soon as we get to Tyre I'll get in touch with the Jew and have him restock our arsenal. I, for one, feel naked without something in reach.

"By the looks of the map, we are about a hundred miles from the Lebanese coastline. Let's take turns at the wheel and try to get some rest. We should arrive off the coast around daylight. The challenge is to avoid leaving a paper trail for Hilda, if she's still around, or for any of the people she works with or works for."

Jake remarked, "We could rent or buy another cruiser and then take this tug out and sink her. If we purchase something for cash and throw in a little extra something for the paperwork to be lost for a month or so, we won't have a trail. We don't know how or from whom Hilda rented the tug."

"Let's throw in the towel for now and take this up in the morning. I'll take the first watch. You guys can draw straws for the who's next," suggested Quint.

The port of Tyre looked the same as it must have a thousand years ago. The only difference was the size and shape of the multitude of vessels crowded into the harbor.

Jett said, "It won't be a problem to find a suitable cabin cruiser, but a shame to sink the Nordic Tug. Maybe we can make a deal to trade the tug and keep it off the books for a reasonable time. Our business shouldn't take more than a couple of weeks on the outside. My friend the Jew should be able to fix us up."

Jake guided the tug through the maze of pleasure craft and small commercial fishing vessels as he looked for a suitable anchorage. Once they dropped anchor, they could take the skiff and head to the beach to find the Jew. They would need to get things moving, for there was little time to prepare for such an ambitious mission.

Quint yelled out to Jake, "Pull in between those two old freighters on our port. We'll drop anchor there and be somewhat out of sight. Jett, if you'll call your friend, we can meet him wherever and see about a boat and the weapons we need."

Jett punched in the Jew's number and waited for the old guy to answer. The cell made some strange sounds, but the sound of a man's voice came through. "International Traders." The voice didn't say any more, just waiting for whoever called to state their case.

Jett responded, "This is Jett Horn. May I speak to the Jew, please?"

The voice yelled something unintelligible, and then the sound of a cranky old man came on.

"Jett, my old friend, how are you? Long time no see. Whenever I hear from you, there seem to be headlines in the papers. What have you in store for this old heart?"

Jett smiled. He could see the old guy standing in his warehouse of amazing stock. "I, sir, am in need of your expertise, and we all should have a heart as old as yours. How are you these days?"

The old guy was slow to speak, but clear as a bell with his words. "I'm just old. What the hell do you want? You didn't come from places unknown to shoot the shit with me. What expertise could I possibly have that you'd be in need of?"

"It's nice to hear such a charming aficionado trying very hard to run off one of his best customers. With all the jesting aside, I and my fellow team members have a very important mission to complete here in your part of the world. It is serious business we're on, with worldwide implications. We'll need some exotic weapons, high explosives, and a fairly large cabin cruiser to house the team. In the mix is a Nordic Tug we need to hide for a couple of weeks. There is a small itch we can't scratch, because a former member of our team may have been a double agent. With your connections on the street, maybe you'll hear something of a blond German woman with Islamic sympathies on the loose here in Lebanon. She'll be looking for the tug and its crew. That will be us."

"Where are you, my friend?" asked the seasoned gunrunner.

Jett didn't hesitate to reveal their position to the old guy, trusting him completely. "We have the tug anchored in the harbor of Tyre."

There was another pause with chatter in the background. "Jett, I have moved my warehouse to Sidon, so we're not far from you. Give me a call when you reach the beach, and I'll meet you with a car. We'll take a ride, and you can tell me what you need besides another boat. I'll put the word out about the blond woman. If she's out there, I'll know before too long."

The cell went dark.

"The Jew says he can help us, no problem. He said to call when we decide what we need besides the boat. He has his antenna up for word of Hilda," related Jett.

Quint brought up the need to recon the sites where the meetings and quarters of the targets were supposed to be held and suggested, "Let's wait to contact the Jew until we do our recon. Maybe check in with him tomorrow. We'll go ashore and check things out first. We could be blowing smoke; maybe the mission isn't even feasible."

Jett began to pace back and forth as though he were ready to take a lap around the deck of the tug. "Let's stop and think about what we have here. Hilda may or may not be our potential nemesis at this point, but we don't know. We have to take precautions in the event she's out there. She has knowledge of what we're up to and the targets. I think we should either hit them after the meetings or before. That way it will be a surprise to anyone privy to our movements. Maybe the Jew will have information on the meetings. He always seems to know everything that's going on in this part of the world."

The three looked at each other and nodded agreement with the new path.

Quint said, "Let's go ashore and take a look at the target locations; we may follow through with the original plan. Jake, you stay aboard and do some healing."

Quint thought about what he'd just said and remarked, "You know, as I think about going ashore, we might want to avoid any locations in the mission plan. We don't know if it's the plan that originated with our employers or one switched by Hilda. She is the handler for this mission and had access to anything she wanted. This whole fucking assignment could be fubar!"

Jake tended to the skiff, lowering it to the water, while the tug was protected by the two old freighters on either side. The water was calm in the diminishing daylight, and the traffic was beginning to slow. The skiff was nearly as big as some cabin cruisers, with plenty of room for the two-man shore party.

When the skiff hit the water, Jett suggested, "We might get in touch with the Jew first thing and see what he's found out, if anything. I think you're right, Quint, we need to steer clear of locations in the plan she presented to us."

"We'll be back sometime tonight or in the morning. If you have a problem give us a call and we'll do the same," Quint instructed Jake.

Quint released the crane hook from the choker lines and easing the throttle forward, he headed for the beach, dodging large and small craft in the process.

While Quint captained the skiff, Jett got on his cell and punched in the Jew's number.

The cell announced itself six times before it was answered. "International Traders." The Jew's Irish brogue came through loud and clear. "You know, Jett, changing your cell now and then might save your life!"

Jett responded, "With the recent events, a new cell phone was the last thing on my mind. We have some major issues to deal with, but with your help we might be able to overcome all the negatives thrown at us."

The Jew wasn't used to any sniveling from Jett. He suggested, "I know a Rabbi who will let you cry on his shoulder. Damn, Jett! What the hell is so important?"

"We have a very ambitious project in the works that may have been compromised from the get-go. It's all about the blond German and the arrival of some three or four heads of state for a secret meeting, if there is such a thing as a secret with such high-profile individuals. If you could put your best street people out there with their ears to the ground, maybe they could shed some light on our situation. We're not sure about the information given to us. Locations, names, dates, times, and such can't be trusted. So what do you think?"

"You get your ass ashore pronto. I can give you some of the information you desire right away."

The cell went dark.

Jett, trying to balance himself against the movement of the skiff, yelled over the noise of the engine to Quint, "The Jew says he can help us right away. Seems whatever we're doing here is not much of a secret."

As Quint guided the skiff into the empty space at the dock, the Jew and his entourage could be seen walking towards their berth.

Jett jumped onto the dock and tied off the bow line as Quint brought the stern into the wooden piling. When Jett stood and turned around, the Jew was there to greet him. They embraced and shook hands.

The Jew remarked, "You look like shit, my friend. Life has not been good to you it appears, and your friend here doesn't look any better. You said there were three of you?"

In the Name of Justice

144

Chapter Ten

Boarding Party

Jake watched the skiff as it maneuvered its way through the throng of shipping in the harbor. His wounds were still tender, but manageable under the circumstances.

His concern was the profile of the Nordic Tug. It stood out like a camel in a bowling alley. If Hilda was out there somewhere, she'd have no trouble finding the tug and they wouldn't have a clue if she was near.

Putting those thoughts aside, Jake began to layout defensive alarms just in case there was a boarding party on the agenda.

After all the pleasantries were over the Jew suggested, "Let's head back to the beach. I have transportation to my warehouse and some interesting news for you. Is your man on the tug in any better shape than you two?"

Quint was slow to answer, thinking of the pain Jake was in and how vulnerable he and the tug were. "Jake, the guy on the tug, is recovering from a few bullet holes and some shrapnel wounds. He'll call if there's a problem."

The growing group headed back down the dock, Jett and Quint in the middle following the Jew, with his bodyguards bringing up their six.

The Jew's warehouse was near the waterfront, with easy access to shipping. They pulled into the huge metal building, hiding their vehicles from roving eyes.

Once inside the warehouse, the vehicles secured, and the huge door locked, the Jew began to share his recent intelligence. "Now that we're all gathered here I have some news to share. Your suspicions were correct about the blond German. She appeared here yesterday and disappeared just as quickly. Hilda evidently has good connections to be able to vanish as she did. My people are still in the streets, and we'll know more in the morning. As for the important meeting and its participants: they're already here. Their get-together is scheduled to take place in two days. The location for their meeting is still not known. We're working on that also. If we can find out by tomorrow, will that be enough time to set things up for your hit?"

Quint and Jett just looked at each other and shrugged.

Quint responded, "Damn! That isn't much time. I suppose the location will dictate our timetable. If it's friendly, maybe we can get it done quickly. If not, then we may think about using an air strike instead of sniper rifles. We do have a few connections for something from the sky."

The whole group seemed to be in a quandary about the next step. Jett filled in the quiet moment. "Let's find out the locations before we get our lingerie in a lump. We're all skilled here, and nothing can possibly come up we can't handle. I say let it go for now. We need to call Jake immediately and inform him that Hilda is on the loose. He might want to take some extra precautions with the tug. It won't be hard to find once Hilda begins to search in earnest. So far, her plans have turned to shit, and I bet she's pretty pissed off right now and looking for vengeance. You know—a woman scorned!"

Jake was sitting on the bow of the tug when he heard a faint splash coming from midships. He turned and limped towards the noise, hoping it was just a fish out of water. As he bent over to shine his flashlight on the water below, he heard footsteps to his left, but he was too late to respond. The blow hit him near the temple, and the stars and stripes played as he hit the deck. He could hear the voice of a woman. "Leave the SOB for now. Start putting the explosives in the places we discussed. When you're finished, we'll tie this asshole's legs and hands and throw him overboard. Check his cell for any numbers that match this area."

Jake tried to lie as still as possible while they searched him for his cell. After they pulled it from his pockets, he rolled over the side of the tug, and splashed into the harbor waters.

Using what strength there was left in his body, he swam underwater to the stern, gulped some much-needed air near the prop and swam toward the bow. Once there, he could use the anchor chain to keep himself underwater and find his way to the surface for more air as needed.

After swimming over forty feet underwater, he grabbed the anchor chain and pulled himself up for more air. He could see the lights trying to find him around midships and towards the stern. The sound of a woman's voice could be heard over the yelling of the searchers. "That SOB better be dead, or you bumbling idiots will find yourselves at the bottom of the food chain here in the harbor. Now dive into the water and search from stem to stern."

When the swimmers came close to the anchor chain, Jake pulled himself down into the darkness further than the searchers were willing to go. Lucky for him they didn't spend much time around the anchor, and he was able to return to the surface for more air.

When Jake's head broke the surface, he could hear his cell's particular sound announcing a call from the beach. The noise from the cell stopped after six tries, and Jake knew Jett or Quint had a good idea that there was trouble. The blond bitch threw the cell over the side, and it landed on the shield hooked to the anchor chain to keep rats from boarding. Just as it began to slide towards the water, Jake pulled himself up far enough to catch the cell just seconds before it could fall into the Mediterranean.

Holding it above his head, he slid back down the chain and underwater, keeping his hand just far enough above the surface to keep the cell dry.

When he pulled himself up again, he heard Hilda order, "Finish up the connections and let's get the hell off the boat. The shore party will be back here pronto, wanting to know why their man didn't answer his cell. We'll stay just off to the port behind the old freighter, and when the time is right we'll pull the pin on the explosives. The Nordic Tug and its shore party will be confetti."

Jake kept a tight grip on the anchor chain until the lights on the boarding party's boat disappeared into the darkness. Not having much strength left, he tied his belt to the anchor chain to keep from sinking and punched in Quint's number.

The phone rang twice before Quint answered, "What the hell's going on? We tried to call earlier!"

Jake was beginning to feel weak, like he was going to pass out. "Where are you guys?"

"When you didn't answer the call, we decided to load up and get back out to the tug. We'll be leaving the Jew's warehouse in a few minutes."

Jake was exhausted from hanging onto the anchor chain. He was thankful that he had the belt to help keep his head and phone out of the warm Mediterranean water.

Trying to focus his energy, Jake said, "Quint, Hilda paid us a visit. She and her hired thugs have booby-trapped the tug. I escaped over the side, and they believe I've drowned. Their boat just pulled away from the tug heading out towards the freighters on either side of us. I think they're going to the port freighter. I'm sure they have some kind of remote trigger device set up to surprise you when you come out to check on me.

149

"I suggest you find some scuba gear and approach the tug from underwater. Once aboard without being seen, you can dismantle her diabolical scheme. If we're lucky, she'll be impatient and come back to check on her surprise, and in that event we can turn her scheme around and ambush her."

"Where the hell are you, Jake?"

"I'm hanging on by a thread to the anchor chain. I suggest you get your asses out here pronto."

There was a pause, and a murmur of voices came over the cell. "The Jew said he has all we need for an underwater approach to the tug. We'll be there ASAP. You hang on. The Marines are on the way!"

Hilda was standing at the wheel of her cabin cruiser chastising her crew with the venom of a snake. "I don't like loose ends. They usually come back to bite you. It was negligent of you to allow our prisoner to get away. Because you didn't find him doesn't mean he drowned and is at the bottom of the harbor. Even though we found his cell phone, we have to assume he has made contact somehow with his partners. Time will tell! We'll wait until dawn before going back to check out the Nordic Tug once more. In the meantime, keep your eyes and ears open for anything coming from that direction."

Quint whispered to the Jew, "I can see the silhouette of the tug in the moonlight. You can bring the boat to a full stop. We'll get geared up, roll over the side, and find our way to the tug. You hang out here. We'll call if it's clear to come aboard."

Quint moved to the stern of the boat, where Jett was putting on his diving gear and said, "We'd better take an extra tank for Jake in case we can't get aboard."

"No problem, I already have one rigged up. Get suited up, and we'll see what the bitch has put in our path," replied Jett.

When the two divers rolled into the sea, they were only five hundred yards from the tug. They wouldn't have to dive until the tug was less than a hundred yards away.

Jett was following Quint and could see he was heading for the bow of the tug and the anchor chain where Jake was hanging on for dear life.

They came up the anchor chain from a depth of twenty feet, scaring the shit out of Jake who wasn't expecting them to come from directly below. When they broke the surface, Jake, trying to keep his voice down, said, "Jesus, what the fuck's wrong with you guys! You took ten years off my already short life. You could have given me some kind of warning, like swimming up to me where I could see you! Jesus."

Quint and Jett were both trying not to laugh, but not doing a good job of it. Still smiling, they helped Jake into the extra scuba gear. With that accomplished the three turned to swim the short distance to the stern of the tug, where Jake could sit on the existing dive platform. He rested there, while the other two removed some of their diving gear and crawled up to the deck to begin a search of the tug, looking for booby traps and trigger devices.

Quint pointed to the port and then himself, to which Jett nodded and took the starboard. They crawled along the gunwales, starting from the outside of the tug and working their way inside.

It was slow, tedious work, and it took a good three hours to find all the explosives. The trigger devices were separated from the C-4, but not dismantled. They might come in handy with the job that lay ahead of them.

Jett was wiping the sweat from his brow as he piled the C-4 up near the galley. There was enough there to blow up the two freighters the tug was sitting between.

He remarked, "Damn! That bitch must really be pissed to waste all this high-dollar shit, when only one packet would have done the job.

"Fuck her and her motley crew. Let's get an ambush set up for her return. Her curiosity will be her downfall on this one. She'll have to come back and check out the tug when she doesn't see us come aboard."

It was nearing daylight when they lifted Jake up to the deck and placed him in the captain's chair. He slumped down to be out of view of anyone checking out the bridge from afar. The chair would have a good view of the entire boat and he would be their eyes and ears until the expected return of the blond bitch.

Quint and Jett stowed the diving gear and took up positions fore and aft to cover the whole tug when their company arrived.

Hilda stood on the bridge of the cabin cruiser looking through the binoculars at the Nordic Tug as the sun began to shed light on the bay. It was her first opportunity to see the tug clearly since they deposited their surprise for the shore party.

Viewing the tug from bow to stern, she couldn't see any activity. The tug looked as dead as Jake, the one who had fallen over the side.

It appeared at first glance that the tug had not been boarded since their departure the night before. Of course, the obvious was not always what it seemed. Hilda ordered, "We have to check out the tug before there is a surge in traffic. Get the boat underway, and when we get close to the tug, circle it for a closer look. If all looks okay, we'll board her and set up an ambush. They have to come back sooner or later. Let's go!"

When the cabin cruiser approached the tug, Hilda ordered all-stop about a hundred yards out. She put her binoculars on the tug once again and kept going back and forth from stem to stern. After a few minutes, she pulled the boat to the opposite side and did the same.

Hilda spoke to the crew. "I believe there is no one aboard, but there is only one way to be sure. Two of you hit the water; swim over to the tug and climb aboard. Give us a hand signal when you are satisfied there is no one aboard."

There was a splash as two of the crew dove into the Mediterranean, swimming under water as far as possible before coming up for air and then diving back under.

Hilda watched them with her binoculars, hoping they would find nothing on board so she could set up an ambush when Jett and Quint came out to check on Jake.

She watched as the two swimmers reached the tug and climbed aboard from the stern and bow, disappearing into the interior of the tug, searching for anyone aboard.

Jake could see Hilda's boat coming and banged on the hull to let them know trouble was on the way.

Jett and Quint peeked over the railing and saw the two swimmers enter the water; they knew that would be the scout party. All they had to do was wait for the two to board, capture them, find out what kind of signal Hilda was waiting for, and then force them to send that signal. Then they could ambush her when she boarded.

The first intruder was neither quiet nor sneaky, and it was not much of a problem for Jett to get his attention with a knife across his neck—he wilted quickly. Jett put him on the deck of the bridge for Jake to watch and went to help Quint with the other one.

When Jett reached the stern, he found Quint pulling a K-Bar out of the shoulder of the other intruder, who was still conscious and yelling some kind of gibberish.

Quint remarked, "This dickhead thought he was invisible or bullet proof. I don't know which. He didn't want to tell me about any signals they were supposed to use, so I had to stick him.

"They don't have any set signal, just a wave for her to come aboard."

Jett asked, "One or both of them?"

The wounded asshole started his gibberish again, but settled down with the knife moving towards the old wound. His English got better, and he said that only one of them was going to wave at her.

"Lets move him up with the other and get rigged up to take on the bitch and her remaining crew, keeping in mind that we need her alive if possible," continued Jett.

Jake suggested, "Let's just throw some of the C-4 onto her boat when she's close enough and be done with it. The bitch doesn't deserve to take another breath, let alone survive to help her communist buddies join up with the terrorist."

The suggestion was taken with a grain of salt. They all knew they needed to interrogate Hilda and find out who and where her connections were.

As soon as Hilda was taken care of, they would head back to the beach and find out what the Jew had learned about their targets.

Jett and Quint pulled the wounded asshole up and shoved him topside to wave for Hilda to come aboard.

After the signal had been given, Quint put his knife at the throat of the other crew member and asked, "How many men does Hilda have with her?" The man was reluctant to speak, but regained his vocal cords when Jett put a Colt .45 to his temple and pulled the hammer back.

The number five came out loud and clear, several times.

Jake moved out of the captain's chair, and they put the wounded intruder in it to be sure he was seen when Hilda arrived. Intruder number two was taken topside and put on the flying bridge with Jake sitting on the deck just below him pointing a sawed-off shotgun at his crotch, keeping his attention focused on doing exactly as told.

Quint also positioned himself on the flying bridge in order to have the high ground in the coming firefight. He would be able to see Hilda and try to keep her alive.

As Jett was heading down the ladder to take his place near the captain's chair, he looked out to see a cabin cruiser heading for the tug. He took a second look and thought they were going a little fast for the crowded conditions. He grabbed a set of binoculars for a closer look and discovered he couldn't find anyone on the bridge or aft. The boat was not manned.

Jett yelled out, "The boat approaching from the starboard is on a collision course with us. Abandon ship! Abandon ship! We are a sitting duck for a broadside."

They didn't take time to worry about their prisoners. Jake and Quint dove off the port side with Jett right behind. The explosion was horrific. The two boats went up and almost completely disappeared. The debris coming down was little more than kindling, with the heavier objects sinking on impact.

Jake was weak from all the activity and had to be held up when the huge wave swept over the trio as they tried to get further away from the impact area.

The Jew, who was sitting off in the distance, fired up his cruiser and headed for the devastation.

There were small craft coming from all directions to rubberneck the scene and look for survivors.

Quint yelled above the noise to Jett, "Look at all the boats. Shit! We won't know if Hilda will be the one to reach us first!"

Jett responded, "Not to worry. I see the Jew's cruiser coming. He was the first to react, but if she's out there along with the rest, she'll know we survived. Let's have the Jew throw us a towline line and not climb aboard. He can drag us out of the area, and we might fool her if she's watching."

When the Jew's boat came abreast, Jett yelled out what they wanted to do, and the Jew threw them two lines. They tied Jake to one line and themselves to the other. The Jew slowly pulled away from the area, increasing his speed gingerly.

They watched the site of the collision as they made for shore. The debris-laden area was now surrounded by the harbor police and scores of spectators. It was impossible to pick Hilda out of the crowd.

When the boat came into the dock area, the Jew put the dock between the wreck site and his boat, shielding the trio as they pulled themselves up to the stern of the boat.

The boat crew was scanning the confusion with binoculars, but couldn't find any blond Germans. She was now missing again and she'd be trouble until they could take her out.

When the three were finally aboard, the Jew tied the cruiser off and they disembarked. There was a truck waiting to take them back to warehouse.

Jake looked over at his soaked friends and said, "Well, how many lives do you think we have left?"

Quint said, "I think you're using yours up a lot faster than we are. You look like a soaked cat with eight holes punched in his life's ticket. Which means you're running short on a backup with only one hole left. Maybe you should throw in the towel and go lie on a beach somewhere to heal up!"

"Fuck you, Quint, I can still shoot straight, and the thought of finding that bitch and her cronies will give me all the strength I need to hang in there," snapped Jake.

The Jew stepped in on the banter. "I have news of your supposed targets. They are not meeting or staying near the waterfront. They will be meeting in two days at the Great Mosque in Sidon. The meeting place down here is a decoy for the news media. We can be up there in no time to scout the area. As for the German bitch, she has been seen around lately asking lots of questions. We'll be able to track her down. I suppose you want her alive when we get her?"

Jett and Jake smiled.

The Jew continued, "We'll stop off at the warehouse, and I'll get to work finding the bitch. You guys can take a break and get into some dry clothes."

After a change of clothes and some chow, Quint said, to no one in particular, "What the hell is the Great Mosque?"

The Jew looked up from his desk. His nose wrinkled under his mop of white hair. "Don't you guys study history? It's an ancient mosque built in the thirteenth century. It's right on the water and has been taken over by everybody and anybody over the years.

Its walls have been restored to their original condition, and it will not be easy for you to get inside. As you know, Sidon is between here and Beirut. I suggest you find a way to do your thing either before the targets get inside or after they depart."

Quint was watching how painful it was for Jake to change out of his wet clothes. He suggested, "Jake, how about you staying here while Jett and I check out Sidon? You can get some rest, and you can go through the warehouse to pick out any of the weapons that we might need."

Jake was not keen to the idea of staying behind, but he was hurting from his wounds. "I'll have to agree. I do need some extra downtime. I can hang out here and be the communications center. Which brings up the fact we lost all our cell phones in the recent escape from that witch's attempt on our lives."

The Jew overheard their conversation. "I have all the communications gear you'll need right here in the warehouse." He called to one of the warehouse guys to get everything necessary for two in the field and one at the warehouse. Then he continued, "I'll fix up that SUV we had earlier for your transportation. Get ready to go."

Chapter Eleven

The Great Mosque

With brilliant magenta bougainvillea spilling over distant garden walls and tall, stately palms and pink and white oleandar lining the divided highway, the short drive north to Sidon was a pleasant one. It was a perfect day. The late afternoon light danced on the water as the sun neared the end of its daily journey, soon to be extinguished in the emerald waters of the Mediterranean.

Jett kept the SUV at the posted speed limit to avoid drawing any attention to themselves, while Quint was lost in thought. *How could such a beautiful place be rocked by such violence for a hundred miles around? What was so important to those involved that the sound of gunfire and explosions was a necessary daily occurrence? What could one neighbor have that the other wanted that warranted such chaos? It was illogical to keep the area in a constant state of anarchy, no matter whose side one was on. Future generations should be allowed to grow and progress without stepping over dead bodies and land mines,* Quint was thinking.

"There she is," announced Jett as the Great Mosque came into view. "It's huge. Damn, the Jew was right. We might have to figure a way to do this without breaching the place."

They drove past the front and down both sides as far as possible. The rear was not accessible by car, so they parked in the lot by the beach and wandered around like tourists, hoping to find some way to access the rear.

Their options were limited. The builders of the mosque had planned well to defend the structure from all sides. Back in the time of the Crusades when the mosque was built, they'd had a good grasp of defensive tactics.

There was no way to enter from the rear, so they walked back around to the front and crossed the street to sit on the rampart at the water's edge.

Jett, who was sitting with his back to the mosque, wondered how the ancients gained entry. He tried to put himself in the shoes of the attackers. The mosque had been taken many times over the centuries, and they didn't have the tools they have today. "We're overlooking the obvious, Quint. Our thinking is in terms of today, when the mosque should be looked at as if it was six hundred years ago. It wasn't strictly manpower that captured this mosque, or even a siege. There is something there we don't see."

Quint was quick to answer, "Let's mosey over to the local library and see if we can pull up the history of the mosque. If we can't find something there, we could wait till dark and take a peek inside."

While they were sitting on the palisade looking at the imposing walls of the mosque, Jett's cell made its funny noise. "Jett here."

There was a long pause on the other end and sounds of a commotion in the background.

162

"Jett—" Another pause, and then the voice of the Jew. "I have some good news for you. We've located the bitch you're looking for. So far we've not taken any action. What would you like us to do?"

Jett tried not to get too excited as Quint was watching and wondering what the hell the call was about.

"Just keep her under surveillance. We'll be back down there just after dark," Jett responded. Then he asked, "We need as much information as possible about Great Mosque. Do you have any knowledge about the details of the structure?"

"Hell yes! I was on a dig there once, tracing the history of its repairs, which revealed a pretty good timeline of its invaders. It was captured and taken over about every fifty to a hundred years by someone. The Crusaders were big on taking over mosques. What can I tell you about it?"

"We'll talk when we get back. Thanks—and you were right about how difficult it would be to get inside and do our thing. See you this evening." The cell went blank, and Jett explained the situation to Quint with a smile. "I think we should take care of Hilda first and then worry about the other targets. She can fubar our mission anytime she wants."

With the last vestiges of the sinking sun they decided to head back down the coast to Tyre and find out where the Hilda was. It would best serve them to take her down as quickly as possible.

Her Lebanon contact was yelling across the bow of the boat, "They are all dead! We saw them on the boat, and they didn't get off. Your plan worked well, Hilda. Don't be so negative."

Hilda was still not positive without seeing some remains, but that was impossible with the horrific explosion leaving nothing but a scattered mass of tiny pieces.

They cruised over the debris for hours trying to find something—anything—to confirm that the three were dead, with no luck.

Hilda ordered, "Captain, take the boat back to the beach, and we'll gather at the villa for another meeting to decide our next course of action. We have to assume they are alive and act accordingly. We'll spend the night in the villa and then take a ride up to Sidon to be sure the meeting environment is safe."

When Jett and Quint pulled into the Jew's huge warehouse, it was apparent that Jake had been busy in their absence. He had all the weapons and explosives they might need for any encounter laid out in neat rows on the warehouse floor. There were any number of options for them to select from, be it for day, night, or in between.

"The Jew told me about Hilda before he called you, and I suspected we might be going on a night raid. As you can see, we have some of the best night vision equipment on the planet at our disposal. What the Jew has in this warehouse would make the CIA or the former KGB jealous.

"I have the layout for the villa where the bitch is staying. It won't be a piece of cake, but we can take her down tonight. We might even be able to give her a long distance-tap. That Modified Remington 700 standing up against the wall over there is mounted with the red dot ACOG: Advanced Combat Optical Gunsights. Then again we could take half the villa out with the Barrett .50 cal sniper rifle. Or could be, you want to take her up close and personal with a fine-wire garrote." Jake was excited and obviously feeling much better as he displayed their choices.

After Jake showed them the weapons, he put a map on the table showing the section of the city where Hilda was holed up. He pointed out the villa in the middle of a short block. She had chosen well, with escape possible from either end of the block or out the rear of the villa.

Jake said, "The Jew has a guy watching her place, and he'll keep us updated until we get our asses over there. It's not far, maybe twenty minutes."

As they studied the map, Jett remarked, "We can't expect the Jew to provide us with any manpower. He's done enough already. We'll have to do this with just the three of us.

"I believe we should take her and her cronies down without any firearms. We can use any number of silent devices. Maybe a blowgun, a garrote as mentioned before, or just deadly force with our hands."

Jake and Quint agreed. Taking Hilda and her crew out face to face would bring the episode to a close.

They had begun to dress all in black, when the Jew's stakeout guy called in that Hilda and her guys were all in the villa except for one guard out front and one in the rear. He thought they were settled in for the night, because they had locked their SUV in the garage, and all the lights were turned off.

Quint parked their vehicle two blocks from Hilda's villa. After a short walk, they spread out to check out the villa from all sides, then waited for a full hour to see if there was a pattern with the two guards.

When the hour was up, the guards hadn't moved, and they didn't seem all that alert, so Quint signaled for a meeting down the street.

"Listen, I'll go around back and take the guard out there. Jake, you stay back and wait for my signal to come forward. Jett, you take the one out front. We'll set the guards up in the same position they're in now, so nothing will look out of place," enjoined Quint.

By now it was nearly pitch dark. They found their way to the villa. Quint moved around back first, while Jett waited to give him enough time to get in position. Jake waited across the street out of sight, hoping all went well and nothing screwed up the plan. He only wanted to see Quint flash his light to bring him up to the building.

Jake could barely see Jett as he garrotted the guard out front. The man didn't make a sound as he fell to the ground. Jett picked him up and set him back on the porch like nothing had happened.

They hadn't brought anything but hand tools and pistols; Jake hoped a gun fight was not in the cards, because they would be horribly outgunned.

Just as Jett was propping up the stiff, the front door opened and out came the guard's relief. They hadn't waited long enough for the guard change. Jett jumped to one side of the porch pillar as the new guard said something to his teammate. When he didn't answer he pushed him, thinking he was asleep.

The dead guard fell over and landed on the sidewalk leading up to the porch. The relief guy had just spent his last moments in the here and now: Jett hit him across the back of the head with his pistol and followed up by twisting his neck around so quickly that he died instantly.

Jake couldn't decide if he should wait for Quint's signal or not, but decided the guard out back was being relieved at the same time and chances were Quint was busy with two guards as well.

He ran across the street to help Jett, who was dragging the body back up to the porch. Jett whispered, "Jake, go around and help Quint. I'll stay here in case someone comes out or tries to escape this way. If I don't hear from you in a few minutes, I'm going to enter the villa and find the bitch. We need to end this tonight."

167

Jake gave a thumbs-up signal and headed around back to find a huge guard and Quint in a life-and-death struggle. They were making serious noise, and the lights came on in the villa. Jake ran up to the back of the huge guard as he had Quint around the neck and was about to finish him. He put his Ka-Bar along the side of the giant's neck and cut his carotid artery. The man didn't fall right away, but he let loose of Quint, who was about to pass out. The big guy started to turn to see what had taken his life force, but instead collapsed, dead to the world. Blood was shooting all over the place, as more guards came out the back door. Quint grabbed the dead guard's AK-47 and let loose with a full magazine, killing the first two out the door.

When Jett heard the gunfire, he busted through the front door and ran smack into another guard coming out. The struggle didn't last long as Jett hit the guard in the throat with a knife, a hand blow that killed him instantly. He picked up the guard's automatic pistol and started searching the ground floor for Hilda.

Quint stepped over the two dead bodies in the doorway and started looking for more attackers and Hilda.

Jake yelled out to Quint, "I guess all the stealth has gone out the window on this one. We better hurry this shit up before the local authorities arrive, and we all wind up in the hoosgow."

Quint shouted back, "You hang out there in case someone tries to go this way. Hopefully, Jett has come in through the front door, and we have her boxed in."

Jett and Quint met on the first floor, so it was a sure thing Hilda was on the second floor, and there was only one way up from the inside.

Going up the stairs with her waiting to blast away would be suicide. Jett suggested, "I'll go back outside and figure a way to climb up to the second floor. When the shooting starts, rush the stairs blazing away; maybe we can catch her and whoever is with her in a crossfire. Jake can watch the back door."

Quint remarked, "Too bad we didn't bring a couple of hand grenades. We don't have much time before the locals get here."

Jett slipped out the front door as Quint positioned himself at the bottom of the staircase, not showing himself to anyone from above.

Jett climbed up the pillar on the porch to the second floor. Finding the porch roof flat and exposed to anyone looking from inside, he continued on up to the roof, hoping to find a way down into the villa from there. As he walked across the roof to the rear he discovered a hatch-looking box. He lifted the box to reveal a ladder leading down into the villa. Throwing caution to the wind, he climbed down the ladder and found himself in a dark, vacant room.

Jett could see light coming from under the door, so he walked quietly towards the door. Just as he reached for the door handle, the door opened and a dark figure entered the room. Jett decided it was time to get the ball rolling and fired point blank into the dark figure. As the figure fell, Jake rolled through the open door, firing in both directions.

Gunfire was coming up from the first floor. Two people who had been trying to go back downstairs fell backwards, and a third bounded down the hall taking a door leading to the back of the villa.

He followed the third person and reached the door just as it slammed shut. He fired a couple of rounds through the closed door and then kicked it open. As he entered he could see the open window. The room was empty.

Gunfire continued from below, so Jett figured whoever had jumped out the window was targeted by Jake.

As Jett climbed cautiously out the window, he could hear sirens in the distance. It was time to get out of Dodge. He yelled down to Jake to head across the street behind the villa, and he'd get Quint and meet him at their car.

Jake yelled back up, "Okay, but I don't see the bitch among the bodies starting to pile up."

Jett responded, "I'll go back inside and down the stairs. See you at the car."

Stepping over the bodies at the head of the stairs, Jett yelled to Quint, "I'm coming down!"

There was no response, so he slowly worked his way down the stairs to find Quint out cold at the bottom, with a flesh wound on his forehead. There were three dead on the floor next to him. He shook Quint to bring him around.

Quint said, "Jesus, the bitch and these three rushed me from under the staircase. I don't know how the hell they got there. The last thing I remember was seeing Hilda running out the front door. The SOB got away again! Shit."

Jett pulled Quint to his feet and said, "We have to get the hell out of here. The local fuzz is on the way. We'll go out the back and catch up with Jake at the car."

They staggered out the rear door and across the back yard to the next street over, where they found their way back to Jake. When they drove past the street leading to the villa, it was jammed with emergency vehicles. Their escape hadn't been any too soon.

The Jew, after securing the warehouse door, remarked, "You know, Jett, you guys remind me of the Keystone Cops in the silent movies. How the hell could you fuck up capturing or killing a person confined in a building? Jesus!"

Quint responded, "They had a secret stairwell we didn't know about. We killed everyone except the German. It will take her some time to regroup and get back on track. In the meantime, we'll continue with our mission and deal with her before we leave."

Jett went on to explain to the Jew that they had found the Great Mosque impenetrable except through the main entrance. They couldn't very well use that without exposing themselves and thus eliminating the advantage of surprise.

As their discussion about what would work and what wouldn't began to grow more heated, there came a feeble voice from the rear of the warehouse.

Sitting in a wheelchair was a bone-thin old man. He was waving at the Jew, who walked to the back and pushed the old man up to the front to join in the debate.

He introduced the wheelchair-bound man. "Gentlemen, I would like to present my uncle. He's a warrior from the past, a hundred years old and still kicking. He thinks the answer to your problem is something he can help you with."

The old man could barely be heard as he whispered and made motions for them to show him a picture of the mosque. The Jew put an enlarged photo of the mosque on the planning table next to the wheelchair.

The centenarian took the pointer from the Jew and indicated the seawall some hundred yards from the mosque.

The old man's lips were moving but nothing could be heard. Quint leaned down close to hear the raspy voice say, "When I was nothing but a boy in short pants, we used to play near the wall there in the picture. One day, when my friends and I were swimming in the area about fifty yards out in the shallow water, we stumbled upon a cave opening in about six feet of water. I think years ago it was above the water level. We waited for the tide to go out the following day and returned to the cave opening. It was pretty much covered by seaweed. If you weren't looking for it, you would never see it."

The old man asked for some water as he rested before continuing his journey into the past.

After a few minutes he resumed his story. "We climbed into the cave entrance and crawled nearly a hundred feet into the darkness. It was not a natural tunnel. It had been man-made in ancient times and knowledge of it had been lost over the years. We were scared to go any further and came back out. One of the boys with us suggested that it would lead into the mosque and probably was used as an escape route when the mosque was under siege by any of the many invaders over the centuries.

"We let it go at that, and I haven't been back there since. You might want to check it out. It could be a way for you to enter the mosque without announcing your arrival."

The old man was now totally exhausted and asked to be pushed back to his spot in the rear of the warehouse.

The Jew wheeled him back and returned, saying, "The old man wishes you well."

Jett looked over at the Jew and asked, "Do you have any diving gear in this amazing warehouse?"

"Hell yes! And the diving boat to get you there."

The Jew had his people gather up enough diving gear for three divers and load the equipment into the SUV.

Quint checked the tide schedules and decided they would dive at first light to check out the old man's story.

Rolling off the back of the dive platform, they checked their gear and began to search for the cave entrance. The water was fairly clear and they discovered the old man's recollections were right on. With little effort they found the cave entrance.

With the diving boat in the area described by the centenarian, the captain threw out the anchor to keep their position while Jett and Quint finished getting into their gear. Jake also suited up to be on standby in case there was a problem.

Quint swam into the dark tunnel, stopped near the entrance, and popped a flare to light his way. He was surprised to see how large the opening and the tunnel were. The tunnel climbed towards the beach. It was easy swimming. With Jett following close behind, they had only gone a hundred yards when they broke the surface into a huge cavern.

Across the cavern and above the waterline, the tunnel continued on up towards the beach and the mosque. As they pulled themselves up to a dry dock sticking out from the tunnel entrance, they spotted two more tunnels on either side, taking the water to who knows where.

Jett said, "Damn! Let's take the gear off and find out where the tunnel goes. Jesus! It's big enough to drive a tank through. If the old-timer and his buddies had gone just a little further, they'd have found this mother of a tunnel. I'm sure he was right about this being an escape route from the mosque and that it was not underwater in those days. They would escape at night or bring in food to wait out a siege. Who knows?"

"Lets get going before we run out of light. These sticks don't last forever," interrupted Quint.

Walking up the slight incline towards the mosque, they were amazed at the condition of the walls. Whoever had been responsible for constructing the escape tunnel was a master of his trade.

The incline became steeper the closer they got to the mosque, ending at the base of a spiral of wide steps winding their way upward.

With Quint leading the way, they took the steps two at a time. The steps abruptly ended at a blank rock wall. They couldn't see any way to enter the mosque. It was a dead end.

"This is total bullshit. This tunnel had to have an entrance or exit!" said Jett, very irritated.

Quint retorted, "Slow down, Jett. Let's take a good look around. We're overlooking something that is probably very obvious to anyone who knows their way around."

The flare sticks created eerie shadows on the walls of the tunnel, leaving a dark spot at any uneven part of the surface, casting doubt on what they were actually seeing.

Quint stumbled over a rough spot near the face of the wall and fell into a dark shaft. He landed with a thud on a shelf about four feet down. He had dropped his flare, which lighted a staircase going down another ten feet. The flame of the flare was moving upwards and side to side, which meant there was a draft coming from somewhere. There had to be access to the surface.

Quint yelled up to Jett, "I believe I have found our way. We were looking for something going up or at our level, not down. I think if we follow the stairs, we'll wind up in the basement of the mosque. Take the steps and bring your light."

The two spelunkers used the steps to reach the diminishing flare that lay on the tunnel floor.

Turning in the direction of the draft, they found a steel door nearly the size of the tunnel itself.

Upon closer inspection, it was discovered there was a smaller door in the center. It was secured with a huge lock that had to be hundreds of years old. The salt air had not been kind to the door or the lock. Quint, using a large stone from the tunnel floor struck the lock. His blow wasn't necessary, for the door cracked open with the lock intact. The latch holding the lock had separated from the rock wall. They gave the door another shove, and it creaked open a little further, leaving them enough space to slide into a large empty room behind the portal.

"Jesus Christ," exclaimed Quint. "Will you look at that. Damn! No one has been here in centuries."

Sitting at a wooden table were two skeletons, still dressed in the armor worn by knights during the Crusades. Just behind the ancient knights was another door, similar to the one they'd just passed through. It was much smaller and didn't have a lock on it.

Walking past the two crusaders, Jett said, "I wonder why they just sat down and died?"

Quint, who was closer said, "They both have broken necks. Maybe their helmets were too heavy. Who gives a shit? They give me the creeps. Let's check out the door and get the hell out of here."

The second door opened with ease, leading them into another, smaller room. Once inside they discovered two hallways going in opposite directions.

Jett said, "Let's take the one on the right and see where it goes; then we'll take a look at the other one."

As they walked down the hall it became apparent it was going in a circle; in minutes they wound up back where they had started.

"Okay, let's start over and take a closer look at the walls as we go," suggested Quint.

On the second walk-through, they used their hands to feel the walls for an opening.

Suddenly Quint grabbed Jett by the shoulder. "Stop!" His hand had moved a wooden plate and light was coming through.

Peering through the opening, Quint found himself looking down on the main chamber of the mosque.

"Hell's bells! Will you look at that? We have a balcony seat overlooking the whole interior of the mosque. If those guys are meeting in here, we have the perfect spot for sniping and a secure exit. Damn! They probably think they are as safe here in this mosque as they would be in their palaces. This will be like shooting fish in a barrel."

The mosque was empty. They kept searching and found a door leading to another spiral stairway and down into the mosque's interior.

With as much stealth as possible, they worked their way to the main floor and the door leading to the gated courtyard and highway.

Jett, asked, "Well, what do we do, my friend? Fall in with the tourists who will be touring the courtyard or go back the way we came?"

"Let's retrace our steps and head back to our diving gear and return to the boat. We shouldn't take a chance on being discovered. I wonder why no one has been down in the bowels of this place for hundreds of years?"

Jake, waiting on the boat's diving platform, was relieved to see the two divers finally break the surface. "It took you guys long enough. We figured you bought the farm. Where the hell have you been?"

"To make a long story short, we discovered the mother lode. If the meeting is still scheduled to be in the Great Mosque, we're in the catbird seat," replied Quint.

The Jew was there to help them aboard and suggested they move the boat as soon as possible. They were drawing attention to themselves by staying in one position so long. Everyone in these parts was paranoid about anything that even hinted of something out of the ordinary.

When they were safely inside the warehouse the Jew said, "I have news of your German woman. She's holed up in a small hotel down near the waterfront. The word is she has some wounds from your last encounter."

Jake jumped in, "I would enjoy taking care of this little problem. You guys can plan the hits in the mosque, and I'll take the bitch out."

Chapter Twelve

Auf Wiedersehen

Jake prowled through the weapons available in the warehouse and selected a Colt .45 and a garrote. He would also take the short blowgun he brought with him from Blaine. He wanted to be up close and personal when he killed the traitor. She had been responsible for nearly killing him on two occasions, and he wanted to look her in the eyes when she took her last breath.

The Jew provided him with a small Triumph motorcycle and directions to the waterfront hiding place where Hilda was recovering from her wounds.

Jake mounted the cycle, yelling over the engine noise to Quint and Jett, "I'll be back sometime in the next 24 hours, depending on how I kill the bitch. If I don't show by daybreak tomorrow, don't come looking for me; just go ahead and take care of business."

He pulled away with a cloud of blue smoke trailing from the old bike. It made very little noise as it disappeared into the night.

Riding down the paved street towards the waterfront in the dead of night took Jake back to another time and place: five years ago in a similar city with a mission to take out a terrorist leader who had been responsible for the death of a high-ranking American diplomat. The terrorist, known only as "Khan," had been betrayed. The people who gave up his location were the relatives of a person Khan had killed. They were more than willing to see him discovered and sent to hell. Jake had been given the assignment to take Khan out with all possible prejudice.

On a pitch black night like this one Jake had set out to take down Khan, who was staying at a condo in a crowded beach area of the city. Jake had found the address purely by accident. It was raining hard, and the streets were beginning to flood. The motorcycle he'd stolen to get to the beach became useless long before he stumbled upon the condo.

Standing under the canvas awning of a small coffeehouse, Jake watched the condo entrance and the windows on the street side. Khan was supposedly in one of the street-side kitchenettes near the middle of the third floor.

All the windows on the third floor were lit except one. Jake stepped into the coffeehouse, ordered a cup of their finest, and sat down by a window that gave a good view of the building. It was supposed to let up with the rain shit soon, so he decided to wait until it stopped. On his third cup the rain stopped, and the flooding in the streets began to subside. Leaving some money on the table, he crossed the street and entered the condo. The elevator proved to be disabled, so taking the stairs was his only option. The condo was near a hundred years old, and every step was an adventure in sound.

He walked down the hall, checking the light under each door, until he came to the only one that was dark. Standing to one side of the door, he listened for any sound coming from within. Not hearing anything, he had to assume there was no one home or whoever was in there was asleep. Then again, Khan could be on the other side of the door listening and waiting for someone to enter.

Turning around, Jake headed back down the hall, down the stairs, and out of the building. He walked back over to the coffeehouse. Sitting back down near the window, he ordered another cup of strong coffee and waited for a sign of Khan coming or going.

The wait was not long; before the waiter brought his coffee, Khan walked out the front door. Standing near the entrance, he looked up and down the street and then walked towards the waterfront docks.

Jake gave Khan a head start before putting a few coins on the table and leaving the coffeehouse. He was hoping for an opportunity to take him out before daylight, when the waterfront became busy with a new day of commerce.

Khan stopped at a warehouse not two blocks from the condo. He knocked on the small door next to the floor-to-ceiling roll-up. The door opened, and he disappeared into the dark interior.

Jake noticed that he'd knocked with a deliberate three and then two raps on the door. Walking around the warehouse, Jake tried to find another entrance or windows to peer inside, but the only access was the front door, so he climbed up a fire ladder to search the roof.

The roof had four skylights painted black. Taking out his Swiss Army knife, Jake began to scrape the black paint from the skylight, hoping to get a look inside.

Before he had scraped an inch of the black paint, he felt cold steel against his neck. He was told in broken English to turn around slowly.

As he turned around, Jake was kicking himself in the ass for being so careless. Standing over him were two large and ugly men dressed in the local garb. They searched him, taking his weapons, and smiling at the quality they'd just inherited.

The bigger of the two pushed him towards the ladder and held him while the other one descended to the pavement. Jake followed with the big guy behind him nearly stepping on his hands as they made their way down.

The trio walked around to the front door and after the appropriate raps they entered the warehouse, to find Jake's mark standing near a chair with straps on the armrests. He knew he was in for a world of shit if he didn't do something before they restrained him. Looking around for a way to fight back he noticed a box of smoke grenades sitting next to a table with pistols of various caliber scattered about on it.

Taking the only opening he might have, Jake head butted the big guy, holding him from behind, while hitting the guy to his front in the throat. With the confusion in high gear, he dove to the floor and rolled next to the box of grenades. He popped one and threw it at the group as they stumbled over each other trying to reach him. The smoke gave him just enough time to grab a couple of the pistols and magazines before the shooting started.

Diving behind a row of tall green lockers, Jake discovered that in his haste, he had picked up clips that didn't match the pistols. Now he was in a one-sided gunfight. Bullets were coming in every direction as the bad guys sprayed the area to their front, punching big bullet holes in the lockers.

Crawling along the floor and keeping his head down, Jake bumped into a box filled with M14s. Taking one of the old rifles out, he discovered it had a full magazine locked and loaded. Trying not to panic with the rounds flying overhead, he secured two more magazines and crawled down to the end of the aisle. Peeking around the last locker, he saw Khan and two of his team crouching behind the pistol table and a box of hand grenades.

Just as he was about to let loose with a burst, he heard the awful sound of a hand grenade bouncing just to the right of his position. It rolled within arm's reach before it stopped at the base of the locker he was lying behind. With the skill and agility of a gymnast, Jake grabbed the grenade and tossed it back to the thrower. It was in midair as it exploded, sending a shock wave in both directions. Thankfully, it was closer to the bad guys. In the confusion of the explosion, he jumped up, moved around the last locker and, remembering the axiom of an old Navy chief—"If in doubt, empty the magazine"—Jake let go on full auto. Between the grenade going off and the .308 rounds hitting their position, the bad guys hugged the floor, giving him the opportunity to move around behind them.

He stationed himself behind four large boxes, a perfect position to take out what was left of Khan and his teammates. After putting in a fresh magazine, Jake rested the rifle on a box. He had Khan in his iron sights. Just as he was about to pull the trigger, he noticed the label on the box: C-4. His blood froze: he was sitting next to enough high explosives to reduce the warehouse to ashes.

Acting on instinct, he searched the boxes for the fuses needed to ignite the C-4. The fuses were inches from the C-4. The Occupational Safety and Health Administration would have a fit over that one! Jake pulled out the fuse with the longest time potential and inserted it in the middle of the huge box.

Looking over his shoulder, he could see the small door that he'd come through in the beginning—it was still open. He pulled the pin on the fuse and retreated to the door on the double with a hail of gunfire following him. Hitting the deck as he neared the door, he rolled through without being hit. Jumping up, he slammed the door shut, put the lock back on the latch, and ran for his life up the block.

Just before he reached the corner of the next building, the explosion caught up with him. The concussion was massive. The warehouse just disappeared. All the windows and doors for two blocks were knocked out, as was Jake.

The shock wave had put him down near a local smoke shop. When he opened his eyes, there was an attractive young woman wiping the blood from his face with a wet cloth. It felt like heaven. Jake moved all his parts and thanked God he was in one piece. The woman helped him to his feet. Still a little dizzy, he headed back up to his hotel to clean up and catch the next flight out of the city. The mission had been completed—no matter the method.

The past was a good reminder to stay alert at all times and not to repeat the same mistakes.

The Triumph was still humming along as Jake made his way towards the address where the blond bitch was holed up. The hit on her would be like the one on Khan—with extreme prejudice.

It was near midday when Jake approached the building where Hilda was staying, a run-of-the-mill place with just a sidewalk between it and the street. It was a good location for surveillance, with a couple of shops across the street to give him cover.

If he couldn't find a way to enter the building without being detected, he'd climb up on the roof of one of the shops and try to reach out and touch her from there. But in that case, he'd have to go back and get a sniper-equipped rifle.

Sitting in a chair in front of the small convenience store was the best way to watch every movement in and out of the building. It wouldn't take long to identify any patterns that would help him find a way to enter.

If Hilda was seriously wounded, she would be ordering out for her meals, in which case he might have an opportunity to become a delivery boy for more than dinner.

It was around lunchtime when the first food delivery took place. A guy pulled up in a small truck that advertised a local restaurant.

Jake hurried across the street as the delivery man was getting his order out of the truck. With the food in a warmer box, he headed into the building with Jake right on his tail. Climbing the stairs up to the second floor, he stopped at the first door on his left, which overlooked the street. He knocked on the door as Jake watched from the corner of the hallway.

She didn't answer right away, then shouted for him to slip his identification under the door, which he did. After a few moments the door opened. She wasn't visible, but her hands took the box, and money was exchanged. They said a few words that Jake couldn't hear. He slipped out and returned to his observation post across the street.

As the driver climbed behind the wheel of the delivery truck, Jake walked over to the vehicle and asked, "Hey, driver, will you be in the area at dinnertime this evening?"

The driver was startled by the sudden appearance of Jake, and responded, "No. I only come to this area for the noon delivery."

Jake thanked him for the information and returned to the shopfront to continue his surveillance of the building. He had decided to wait until dark to send the bitch to her promised land.

The Jew motioned for Jett and Quint to follow him into his office.

"Gentlemen, I have good news for you about the evil empire. The trio of men you wish to help find their way to the virgins have added one to their gathering. He is a thorn from South America. Their meeting is on schedule for the day after tomorrow. It is said they are forming an alliance to bring all the evil empires under one tent. After this mission, you may have only one left to take out—the potbelly. And he doesn't wander far from home."

As the Jew finished his report, Quint remarked to Jett, "You know, we could just fill the mosque with C-4 and make everything disappear in a few moments. It would be a lot easier than taking them out in a gunfight."

The Jew became agitated. "You can't do that! The Great Mosque has been there for centuries. Even though it's not part of my religion, this is a piece of history that goes back to before the Crusades. Some things should be preserved, and that mosque is one of them."

The small office was getting a little crowded with all the tension in the air, so Jett said, "Okay, okay. We're not going to waste the mosque, even though it would be a no-brainer to take the easy way. Our original plan was to take them down with sniper rifles, blowguns, or up close and personal, by cutting their throats. We'll choose one of those."

Jett and Quint left the warehouse and headed back to the Jew's boat to figure out the best way to proceed. With the secret entrance they'd discovered, surprise was on their side.

While they were standing on the stern of the cabin cruiser watching the harbor tide going out, Quint remarked, "You know, Jett, we might be able to take care of our business without ever firing a shot."

"So you want to bring the whole mosque down with some C-4? I was under the impression we'd agreed not to destroy the ancient landmark!"

"No explosives. We'll let Mother Nature take those scumbags out."

"What do you figure on doing, having lighting strike the mosque?"

"No, water. Specifically, salt water."

"You're going to have it rain salt water? I suppose you have some Indian friends who can give us a deluge on demand?"

Quint was having fun with the banter. "We don't need lighting or Indians to do our bidding. What we have is right before our eyes. Actually, we're looking at it now."

Jett was getting a little tired of the game. "Get to the fucking point, Quint. What the hell are you talking about?"

"The tide, man, the tide! As I recall, the meeting room is below sea level. Just above the basement we came up through. It has only one entrance. They must feel pretty safe to put themselves in such a tight spot. But I guess they figure it's the only way they can meet without prying eyes and ears. They feel invincible once they're inside the walls of the mosque. You remember the two waterways that drained the tide back out to keep the tunnel dry?"

"Sure, so what?"

"We could plug the waterways and bar the meeting room door. The tide would fill up the tunnel and then run into the mosque and down on them. They drown in the salt water, and we release the plugs and swim away. No one knows but that it was all a natural thing. The next day we read in the newspaper about the demise of four world leaders in a tragic accident. A mystery of the Great Mosque."

"This all sounds great and looks good on paper, but I don't think it will be that easy. How the hell do you plan on plugging the waterways? And how about the small problem of blocking the meeting room door so they can't get out?"

Quint was remembering his tour of the Jew's warehouse. It was an army-navy surplus store in the old tradition, but also a storehouse of the new and exotic. What had piqued his interest was the amount of surplus maritime equipment, in particular, the inflatable rubber buoys.

Quint said, "I can block the spillways if you can figure a way to secure the door to the meeting room. We pick up inflatable buoys from the warehouse, put them in the spillway tunnel, and block the water from escaping into the harbor. The water backs up into the mosque. When the deed is done, we deflate the buoys and disappear. Piece of cake!"

"Are you shitting me? The timing for your scheme would have to be perfect, and there is no such thing as a perfect plan. Something will go wrong, and there is no room for error here. What is your backup if the water doesn't reach them on time?"

"That won't be a problem. The tide comes in at a certain rate, and with the volume of the tunnel, it takes x amount of time to fill it up and spill into the mosque. I have figured it all out."

"You still need a Plan Two."

"Okay, if the seawater doesn't pan out, we'll rain a bunch of hand grenades onto the meeting. That

192

would take care of their summit and not inflict undue damage to the mosque. But if we wind up doing it that way we'll bring a lot of heat on the whole world from their disciples. With the water, there is no one to blame. It would appear to be the will of God."

Jett didn't answer right away. Finally he said, "Okay, with that out of the way, how do we secure the door to lock them in?"

"I don't have a clue. I was busy thinking about the tides and spillways. As I recall, the door is metal and a fairly tight fit. It wouldn't leak much even without caulking or something like it. We would need to fuse the metal door to the metal frame somehow, which would take someone being inside the mosque."

"I think Jake may be our answer," responded Jett. "He could take one of the tours, then separate himself once inside and find a place to hide for the night. The day of the meeting there won't be any tours, but he'll be inside. We know the door and frame are metal, so we just need to go back to the Jew's warehouse and find something for him to put between the door and the frame that will fuse the metal."

Quint thought for a while. Then with a big smile he said, "Why not just lock the door and throw the key away? All those old doors had locks, and you have to remember that the mosque was built to withstand invasions, so I would suggest it's a strong door with little chance of breaking it down from the inside without tools."

"Where do we find a key for a centuries old door lock?"

"We might get lucky; it might be sitting in the lock as we speak. When Jake gets back, he can go check it out. He should be back in the morning. I'll bet he's waiting for dark to send Hilda to the promised land.

With the sun taking its last breath before dipping into the Mediterranean, Jake figured it was near time to enter the condo and take care of Hilda. A few bucks to the store owner had kept him from calling the authorities to report loitering and given Jake a little more time to wait for darkness.

It wasn't long before the few street lamps that were actually working started to flicker and come on. Jake made his way across the street and entered the main entrance of the building. Passing up the elevator, he used the stairwell to access the third floor.

The building was old and seedy. The walls were worn. They needed repair, and the floor squeaked with every step, making a sneak attack almost impossible.

Taking measured steps and trying to be as quiet as possible, Jake finally stood at Hilda's door listening for any sounds from within. There no light coming from under the door or from under the doors on either side.

He decided to be bold and knocked. "Pizza delivery."

There was no response nor any sound of movement, so Jake tried the door handle. The brass handle moved as he pushed it down, and the door swung open. Dropping to his knees, Jake crawled into the dark room. Still not hearing any movement, he stood and flipped on the overhead light.

Sitting in a chair near the window was Hilda, dead as dead could be. Her throat was slit from ear to ear. Her beautiful face was not pretty anymore. She had gunshot wounds to her shoulder and hip, which didn't have anything to do with her demise.

Hilda hadn't cut her own throat. Whoever put the knife to her neck did it from behind, just minutes before Jake's arrival.

Turning to get the hell out of the room, Jake saw the shadow too late to take evasive action. The blow hit him on the left temple, and the stars began to shine and flicker in all directions.

Reeling from the blow, he rolled onto the floor, putting his hands up to protect himself from further damage, but even in the fog of the blow he could see the shadow of the assailant dart out the door.

Jumping to his feet with the stars still shining, Jake staggered over to the window to see the killer run out the front and jump into a French Citroen. It took off in a cloud of blue smoke and disappeared into the dark night, just as the local authorities drove up to the entrance with lights flashing. Someone had timed the arrival of the cops to discover Jake out cold at the scene of a murder. Someone had known he was waiting and wanted him found with the body.

Still not clearheaded, Jake grabbed Hilda's knapsack from the table and turning to her lifeless body said, "Auf Wiedersehen, bitch." Leaving the room, he hurried to the end of the hall. Taking the nearest exit, he descended the fire escape at the rear of the building and ran across the alley into the next complex of buildings, leaving the sirens and flashing lights behind.

Stopping on the next street, he managed to hot-wire an old VW and put some distance between himself and the bloody murder scene. He was pissed at not having the opportunity to watch her bleed to death and to thank the guy who slit her throat.

The VW began to sputter and die about halfway to the Jew's warehouse. Whoever owned the car was a cheap SOB and hadn't kept the tank full. Jake left a note to the owner behind the windshield wipers, suggesting he keep the car filled up in case of emergencies.

Hailing a cab, Jake tried to get his head clear before he had the driver drop him a block away from the warehouse. It wasn't good policy to have records of one's whereabouts in this part of the world.

The lights were on in the warehouse when Jake rang the bell on the small door that was used when the roll-up was closed. He was welcomed by Jett and Quint, who were getting their gear ready for plugging the spillways in the secret entrance.

Quint exclaimed, "You look like shit, Jake! What the hell happened to the side of your face? Is the blood from old wounds or new ones?"

Jake walked over to the couch near the Jew's office and took a seat. "Somebody made me while I was staking out Hilda's digs. When I went up to take her out, she was in a chair with her throat cut. When I turned to get the hell out of there, the guy who killed her slapped me upside the head. He thought I was out when he jammed. He had a partner waiting downstairs and they fled. Before they were out of sight, the local cops showed up. It was a setup to blame the murder on me. I was lucky to get out of there. Her own people dumped on her to get to us. So we know they're still out there, and we need to keep a watch on our ass."

Jett interrupted, "You didn't get to say anything to her?"

"I said, 'Auf Wiedersehen bitch.' Which reminds me—here's the only thing I had time to grab."

Jake handed the backpack to Jett, and remarked, "I need to get some rest." He stretched out on the couch and promptly fell asleep.

Quint looked over at Jett and commented, "How the hell do people do that? Just sit down and go to sleep."

"Hell, I don't know. Let him sleep while we check out the bitch's belongings. We'll need him tomorrow for the mosque."

The only thing of value in the backpack was the itinerary of the big three plus one. It was right on the nose with the information the Jew had given them. Who Hilda's cohorts were and where they were was still a mystery.

Putting that aside for the time being, Quint said, "Let's turn in for the night. We're going to be busy as hell tomorrow taking the inflatable buoys down to the tunnel and getting things rigged up for the tide to do our bidding."

Chapter Thirteen

Site Prep

A heavy downpour beating time on the warehouse roof and the smell of coffee provided the incentive for the three amigos to rise and shine.

Jett picked up the local paper as he was downing his second cup of strong Middle Eastern coffee. The headline shouted out the death of a German national from Mexico found murdered in her recently-rented condo near the waterfront. The story went on to say the motive wasn't known, but it was thought the killer had fled the scene just as the authorities arrived at the condo, acting on a telephone tip. The lead investigator reported there were no witnesses to the crime.

Jett threw the paper over to Jake. "Guess you got away clean, along with the killer. Maybe we'll have the opportunity to find him, thank him, and kill him."

Quint chimed in, "Jake, we have a plan to execute our mission on the Axis of Evil. You're going to be put in a little jeopardy. We've decided to use inflatable buoys to plug the spillways. To keep the water and our targets from escaping from the meeting room, we need to secure the only access door from the outside. That's where you come in."

"Look fellows, I'm not a hundred percent, as you can see. Maybe you should consider using one of the Jew's guys for this."

"No chance, Jake," responded Quint. "You're the man. Today you can take one of the tours into the mosque, find the meeting room door, and see if there's a metal key on the outside or inside of the door. If it's on the inside, take it out and put it on the outside.

"When the seawater begins to fill the meeting room, the door has to be locked from the outside. Without tools, they won't be able to break out before the place fills up. When the water rises to the perforated ceiling, it would be possible for one or more to float up and try to escape that way, but the perforations are too small for a person to slip through. However, they are big enough for us to drop some hand grenades through if the water doesn't do the trick. Either way, they are locked in and at our mercy."

"You expect me to walk into the mosque, go snooping around, find the meeting room, change the door keys, and walk out without a how-do-you-do? Are you nuts? The tour people don't allow stragglers to go off on their own. Jeopardy is a lame word for the position I'd be in." Jake gave them a stern look. Then he smiled. "I don't see a problem. When do we start?"

The Jew had been standing nearby listening in on the conference. He had a suggestion. "First thing you better do is put some shades on those blue eyes and dye your hair and mustache black. Then we'll find some local garb for him to wear. If you do that, he might have a chance of snooping around the mosque."

200

Without any further conversation, the group walked over to the maintenance section of the warehouse and began the process of transforming Jake into a local. Within an hour, the blue-eyed, light-haired, mustached Jake had a makeover that gave him the persona of a local middle-class businessman.

"One other thing. I have to go back into the mosque and lock the door from the outside just as the water begins to fill her up! Oh— And keep the bad guys and their aides from interfering. Have I got that about right?" Jake asked as he admired his disguise in the mirror.

Quint answered, "Yeah, that pretty well covers it, Jake, with one exception: you'll have to find a place to hide when the tour leaves. You need to stay inside overnight because there won't be any tours the day of the meeting."

Jake looked incredulously at Quint. "That isn't a Motel 6 for crying out loud. You think they have rooms all made up for overnight guests? Jesus! And you used the word "jeopardy" to describe my situation? How about *suicide!*"

"What the hell, Jake, I'm sure it won't be a pajama party, but we need you in there. Without the door being locked, the whole deal is a bust. It's a great opportunity to let Mother Nature take the blame for ridding the world of the evil empire's amigos."

"Okay, okay, I get the message," Jake responded, and then asked the Jew, "How about another motorcycle for my ride over to the mosque? I can leave it across the street with a hundred others. I promise to bring this one back."

"No problem, my friend," the Jew said, knowing the bike would be stolen or wrecked before he saw it again.

Jake fired up the bike, and looking every bit like a local, headed for the mosque and a long night alone in the ancient structure, which was probably haunted by ghosts from who-knows-what century.

The Jew waved as the truck pulled away from the roll-up door of his warehouse. Jett was sitting in the shotgun seat while Quint was sitting back in the bed of the truck, keeping watch on the diving gear, extra air tanks, and inflatable rubber buoys.

They were not pressed for time to get the equipment down to the waterfront because the tide was just coming in, and the water had to be deep enough for the boat to anchor over the cave entrance.

As the truck turned into the parking lot at the end of the dock access, Quint noticed a mini truck parked across the street with two people in the front and two sitting in the bed of the small vehicle. They seemed out of place somehow, and the hair on his neck began to tickle, a good indication that something negative was in the air.

After the driver pulled up to the end of the dock, he turned around and backed down stopping at the stern of the cabin cruiser. Quint jumped out to begin offloading their gear.

When Jett came around to help, Quint asked, "Did you notice the mini truck?"

Jett nodded. "Those four men don't appear to be stevedores or deckhand types looking for a job. You don't suppose the German bitch is trying to take us down, even from her final resting place, do you?"

Quint was making his last trip to the boat when he remarked, "I think when we finish up here, we'll have enough time to take a walk."

After the truck was offloaded, Jett looked over their small arsenal of weapons and chose two machine pistols with extra magazines. He handed one to Quint as they walked back up the dock to the parking lot, where they turned north.

Stopping at the sidewalk between the seawall and the street, Jett remarked, "They're still sitting there. I don't think they're waiting on an offer for day labor. Let's head up the road and see if they follow."

With a quick step they made the first block in a short time. As expected, the mini truck pulled out onto the main drag and followed them.

Quint was keeping a eye on their six, while Jett was trying to decide where to lead the four soon-to-be-dead stalkers.

As they reached the middle of the second block, Jett turned into a dark, lonely-looking alley. He whispered to Quint, "You get on the left; I'll take the right about twenty yards ahead of you. Open up on them when they turn into the alley. If the truck manages to get past you,

I'll be here to take out the remainder. If they stop, I'll head back and concentrate on the cab, while you waste the truck bed."

"Sounds good to me, but don't you think we should try and keep one alive to find out if they are just the beginning?"

Jett didn't hesitate. "We can't pick and choose who lives or dies. If one survives the ambush, so be it. If there are more of them, it won't matter. In a couple of days we'll be back in Blaine looking for another exciting adventure."

Quint looked at Jett with a smile and said, "Why are you whispering? We are fifty yards from anyone with ears."

"Habit," responded Jett, as he walked past Quint to his ambush position.

Just as Quint took his position, the truck turned into the alley with its lights off, going very slowly as it proceeded in the semi-darkness. Quint noticed as the truck pulled even with him that the two in the cab were the only ones in the truck. Those who had been in the truck bed were most likely running around to the other end of the alley. Quint took the safety off the machine pistol and emptied the magazine into the cab.

The two were dead within seconds. As Quint turned to warn Jett that he should expect two bad guys to hit him from the other end, he saw the flashes from the gun barrels and the sound of weapons going off in rapid fire. He dove to the deck with bullets hitting the wall just above his head and ricocheting off the alley walls.

Rolling over and over until he reached the opposite side, Quint bounced to his knees. In the near-dark conditions he could make out the figure of Jett against the light from the other end.

Not taking much aim, he fired to Jett's left just as Jett let loose. The barrage seemed to work its magic. There was no return fire.

Standing up, Quint ran up to Jett, "Are you all right? Jesus, they put out a lot of firepower. What the hell were they shooting at us with?"

Jett was holding his left arm. Blood leaked between his fingers onto the ground. "Damn, one of the rounds bouncing off the walls came back to bite me. It's not serious. Better go check and see if one of those pricks is still alive."

Walking over to the two bodies lying against the wall, Quint felt their necks for any sign of life. The first one looked like a used-up target in a shooting gallery. The second had a pulse. He turned him over to find a knife looking him in the eye. He was not only not dead, he didn't have a scratch on him. The knife missed his neck by inches as the not-so-dead guy jumped to his feet.

Quint sidestepped another thrust from the poorly-trained assailant and came around with his pistol to catch him on the temple, hoping not to kill him. Down he went like an empty sack just as Jett came up from behind and tried to throw a body block to knock him down. He flew over the man's prone body and landed in a heap in front of Quint.

Quint looked down at the bleeding Jett and remarked, "Nice timing. Did you play college or pro ball?"

Not amused, Jett regained his footing and composure. "Neither. We only had ten guys in our graduating class. How the hell did this asshole miss catching at least one bullet from all that lead flying around here? Jesus!"

"Lucky for us he's still with the living. We might be able to get some information from him about who's paying his salary and why. In the meantime, we better vamoose out of here before the sheriff arrives. We might have a hard time explaining what the hell went on here. I'll go get the truck. We'll throw the bodies in the bed and head back to the dock. We can dump them overboard on the way to the cave."

Quint drove up to Jett, who was standing next to the two bodies. They loaded the stiffs into the truck bed and headed out the far end of the dark alley just as the flashing lights passed the other end. By the time the authorities found out where the gunshots had come from, they'd be back at the dock, and the only evidence left behind would be blood and a few brass casings. There would be no way to connect anyone in particular with the scene.

Arriving at the dock, they backed the truck up to the stern of the cabin cruiser, and the crew jumped down to help them stow the bodies on the deck. The captain told a crew member to take the truck across town, park it in a busy lot, and then return to the Jew's warehouse.

With that taken care of, the captain idled out far enough away from the dock to throttle up. Dodging the ships anchored in the harbor, he set a course for the cave entrance.

"The buoys fit like they were made for this day. Damn!" said Quint. They had put the uninflated rubber balls in place. If their calculations were correct, the tide coming in around midnight would flood the tunnel and begin to spill over into the mosque meeting room around the time that the gathering in the mosque was brought to order.

Jett said, "Well, since the buoys fit, let's go back and start bringing in the extra air tanks. We'll err in favor of having too many rather than run short and not fill the buoys to their capacity."

With the last dive, all the necessary preparations for the tide at midnight were completed. They returned to the boat and waited for word from Jake.

Jake parked his cycle across the street from the mosque and hurried over to get in line with the rest of the tourists for the first tour of the morning. The disguise was perfect: he blended in well with the local and foreign tourists waiting for the tour to start.

Appearing to be just one of the crowd, Jake listened as the guide explained the architecture of the mosque the history of those who built it, and the story of how it changed hands every hundred years or so.

Once the tour entered the mosque proper, he hoped they would pass by the metal door he was looking for and reveal a good place to hole up for the night.

As they walked deeper into the structure, he noticed four tough-looking men standing before a metal door and figured that must be his objective. He dropped out of the crowd, found a short set of stairs leading up to a balcony, and climbed up to observe his target.

Watching for a few minutes, Jake discovered two more men searching the meeting room. That made a total of six so far.

Two of the four outside the meeting room split off and began to search every nook and cranny within the huge interior. The other two stood guard, not allowing anyone passing through to come near their protected area.

After a two hour-vigil, it was apparent they were going to come up the stairs before long, so Jake made his way around the balcony to the opposite side and waited until they had checked out his former position. He then descended the stairs and with great care found his way back up the stairs to his old spot. The men continued around the balcony and down the stairs he'd just come from.

Jake figured that with the view from the balcony and the fact it had now been cleared by the bad guys, he'd spend the night there, keeping an eye on his objective.

Now all he had to do was figure a way to get rid of the guards. If he killed them, it would have to look like an accident. The best option would be to lure them away long enough for the room to fill with seawater. But the immediate problem was to get the key from the inside of the door to the outside and hope no one noticed that the key had been moved. It would probably not be a big deal to them, thinking the door was so old it was only an ornament. With so many guards running around, it would be difficult to make a move, so Jake decided to wait until dark to sneak down and change the key.

Taking out the cell phone, he dialed the Jew's warehouse number, hoping Jett or Quint had returned from the morning dive on the cave.

The Jew answered, "So my friend, you are still among the living?"

"Yes, and I need to speak to Jett or Quint."

"Check the cell phone book. Their number is listed. Is there anything else I can do for you?"

"Not now, thanks. I'll be in touch."

Jake checked the memory bank in the cell and punched in the number for his teammates.

"Quint here. It's about time you called. We're set on this end. What's your status?"

Jake was glad to hear a friendly voice. "I'm waiting until dark to change the key. But I have a small problem. How do I get rid of the door guards when the time is right? If this is supposed to look like an act of God, I can't take them out with earthly means."

The cell was quiet for a time before Quint said, "Do you have your blowgun with you?"

"Yes, I always have it with me."

"Do you have the stuff to put on the darts that will just stun them?"

"Yeah, I get you. I can stun them long enough to switch the key. When they come to, they'll think they fell asleep. They won't be anxious to tell anyone they were out. Good thinking! I'll work on that. Call when you want me to start. I have the phone on vibrate."

The cell went dark, and Jake returned to observing his target.

Chapter Fourteen

High Tide

Quint yelled up to the bridge, "Bring her over the cave; it's deep enough now. We'll suit up and head below."

Jett was on the diving platform at the stern of the cabin cruiser gathering up their gear for their venture back into the tunnel. It would be their fourth dive. It would last until the seawater drowned the Axis of Evil, plus one. The world would be a better place without them in spite of the turmoil with all the wannabes jockeying for position in their countries.

The time would be ripe for the nations who wanted a peaceful world to show some balls and help those who were fighting for their freedom. Those who had been lying low, working in the darkness to rid themselves of dictators would need help. Now they would have the perfect opportunity to free their people of their chains and allow them to breathe the fresh air of freedom.

Quint had jumped down next to Jett and begun to suit up when the captain announced there were two boats on a heading that matched theirs. "Gentlemen, I think we're about to have company, maybe before you can get your equipment on. It might be wise to take battle stations if the boats prove to be hostile. After the fiasco you had ashore, maybe they had friends."

Jett and Quint dropped their diving gear, climbed back up to the main deck, and armed themselves with pistols and knives.

Quint said, "I hope this doesn't take long. We need to use the tide tonight."

When the boats were within fifty yards, they split and went around either side, not even slowing down.

The captain yelled out to the crew, "False alarm."

Jett yelled back, "Not so fast, Captain. I think they mean us harm. Look, they're coming about."

Sure enough, the two boats reversed course and came at them like a couple of suicide planes from WWII.

At the last possible moment, the two boats shut down their engines and coasted up to the cabin cruiser with guns blazing.

The captain was dead in the water with the anchor still dragging. He took cover, ducking under the flying bridge, as most of the firepower was directed at him.

While the crew was returning fire, Jett picked up some hand grenades, tossed two to Quint, and pointed to starboard. Quint took the hint and went to port. The waves from the sudden shutdown of the attacking boats had turned the cabin cruiser between them and jerked the anchor chain straight as a railroad track.

Quint had visions of the German bitch touching them from the grave as he tossed a grenade into the attacking boat. It bounced off the bridge and into the water on the other side as it blew. The second one landed near the stern and blew a nice hole in the deck, which caught fire. The crew members that were still standing didn't fight the fire but kept up the barrage of bullets.

When the flames reached the fuel tanks, it was all over but the shouting. The boat went up in a ball of flame, scorching everything within twenty yards and knocking Quint to the deck—out cold.

Jett dove into the water, coming up on the opposite side of the second boat in time to see the flames and feel the concussion from the first attacking vessel. He used the confusion to slip his first grenade into a porthole just above the waterline. He swam as fast as he could to the stern of the boat, tossing his second grenade onto the deck just as the other went off.

Diving as deep as he could, Jett was still tumbled head over heels when the shock wave hit and pushed him even deeper. Using his last bit of air, he managed to swim for the surface as the blown-up boat passed him heading for the bottom. By the time Jett got to the stern of the cabin cruiser, Quint had found his way to the diving platform, still groggy from the explosion.

The captain had taken a couple of bullets, but he was still in command. He yelled, "Get the diving gear on and disappear. The coast guard will be along in short order, and we'll need to be away from this position. The flames from the boat that didn't sink are a beacon for them to follow."

With all the speed they could muster, Jett and Quint donned their gear and splashed into the water, out of sight within seconds as they descended towards the cave entrance.

The captain cut the anchor loose and got the cabin cruiser out of the area, leaving the burning attacker dead in the water, along with any survivors who may have jumped ship.

With Quint in the lead, he and Jett found the cave entrance and swam up to the tunnel. It wouldn't take them long to fill the rubber buoys and block the spillways.

"Hurry it up! We don't have much time left," said Quint as they filled the remaining buoys with air. "We have to have this finished within the hour. If our calculations are correct, the water will spill over into the mosque at eight thirty tomorrow morning.

"The meeting should be well under way by then. Soon as we finish blocking this last spillway, we'll call Jake and tell him to lock the door as soon as all the participants are inside."

Jett moved the last air tank into position to fill the buoy to capacity. The two spillways were now airtight. The tide would fill the tunnel and eventually the mosque itself. They would have to retreat back to the surface, not having enough air to wait for the high tide to do its work.

When Jake called them to verify that the dictators were indeed dead to the world, it would be time to return, deflate the buoys, and remove the evidence

214

that anything but a freak of nature had saved the world from a clash with civilization from those who would, if given the chance, bring the world to its knees and back to the tenth century.

"That's it, let's head back topside," said Quint as the last of the air tanks was emptied. "I hope the cabin cruiser is back, and the mess we left behind has cleared."

When they broke the surface it was dark, and the boat that was burning when they jumped into the water was being towed by a coast guard cutter towards the harbor.

"Damn! I wonder how long we'll have to tread water until the captain feels it's safe to come back for us?" questioned Jett.

"He wouldn't wait long, but he did have some gunshot wounds that needed attention," said Quint. "Maybe they went ashore, and someone else will come for us."

While they were discussing whether to head for shore with the tide or hang out until help arrived, the dark silhouette of a small craft could be made out heading in their direction. It wasn't moving fast enough to make white water, but moving steadily towards them.

Quint suggested, "Lets separate in case the craft coming in our direction isn't friendly. We would have a better chance coming at them from two sides."

Jett nodded in agreement and they swam farther apart.

The small boat reached the site for the pickup and dropped anchor, indicating friendly skies had arrived. Jett and Quint swam over to the boat and were pulled aboard.

The leader of the crew had news from the Jew. He spoke in a low, quiet tone. "The Jew wants you back at the warehouse. The captain of the cabin cruiser died from his wounds, and the coast guard has been snooping around. He thinks they identified the cabin cruiser and will be asking questions. He's going to say they were attacked by the same people who killed the German girl, and that it was a vendetta from a past deal gone wrong. He'll need your support during the questioning."

"Sure, anything we can do to help. But we have to be back here sometime after eight thirty to finish our work," responded Quint.

"The Jew knows that. He wants to be sure your mission is a success. He's as anxious to rid the world of those despots as anyone else, but he also has to cover his ass. You can leave the area when you're finished—he can't."

When the group returned to the warehouse, Quint got on the cell and dialed Jake's number. On the third ring he heard, "I have to whisper because I'm surrounded by the bad guys. What's up?"

Quint said, "When the last guy enters the meeting room, lock the door. The tide is on the way in, and the spillways are blocked. It will spill over into the mosque at around eight thirty."

"Lock the door? I haven't even switched the key yet. Shit! Okay, I'll have to step it up."

"We have a problem here. As soon as that's cleared up, we'll get back out to the cave entrance and clear the spillways. It's on you now, Jake!"

The cell went blank. Jake put it back in his pocket wishing he had a squad of Marines to give him a hand.

Looking over the balcony rail he could see only one guard on duty, so he slipped down the stairs, around the corner of the meeting room, and put a dart in the man's neck.

Pushing the door open, he grabbed the key, but it wouldn't budge. Twisting and turning the key didn't work either. *Damn! Where's the WD-40 when you need it?*

Going around to the front of the door, Jake put his knife in the old-style keyhole and pushed the key out the other side.

Just as he was retrieving the key from the inside floor, the guard started moaning and began to shake his head, trying clear out the cobwebs.

With the luck of the Irish, Jake got the key into the outside, twisting it a little making sure it was secure, but not far enough to lock it, as the guard began to rise.

The guard's back was to Jake as he turned the corner of the meeting room and scrambled up the stairs to his temporary stakeout position.

The guard tried to get up, but fell back down in a heap, only to try again with the assistance of the door handle, this time succeeding.

He felt his neck and looked around for any sign of trouble. Not seeing anything out of place, he looked into the meeting room and then closed the door not noticing that the key had been moved.

All Jake had to do now was wait for the participants to gather in the meeting room, then dart the guards and lock the door. Piece of cake.

The Jew confronted the authorities when they entered the warehouse. "Hello, gentlemen, how are you? What can this poor white-haired man do for those who protect and serve the people?"

The officer that seemed to be in charge asked the Jew some questions that couldn't be heard and then stepped back.

Turning to his warehouse personnel, the Jew asked, "The kind protectors of the people would like to know if anyone here noticed anything unusual out in the harbor the last couple of days?"

Quint stepped forward and responded, "Yes, our boat was sunk by a German woman and her entourage, and then last night they tried to sink the Jew's boat while we were practicing night diving. She had a vendetta for myself and Jett, my friend here, after a deal with her went bad in Mexico sometime back."

The police officers huddled up, and there was a lot of shaking and nodding of heads as they tried to sort things out.

The lead officer finally said, "The German woman had her throat cut from ear to ear. Her small group of bad guys seem to find themselves dead or wounded on a daily basis. I don't suppose you know about any of those instances?"

Quint shook his head and responded, "Only last night."

The Jew intervened, "They almost destroyed my cabin cruiser, and they killed her captain. We fought back, and you found the results in flames on the water. Another of their craft is at the bottom. We defended ourselves—clear and simple."

The lead officer nodded. "Okay, we'll take another look around, and in the meantime you people stay in the city."

They returned to their vehicles and sped away.

The Jew remarked, "That won't be the last of them. I believe they would like to put me out of business, but I'm not without some influence with the local government. I'll prepare another boat for you to get back out to the cave."

Quint and Jett showed visible signs of relief when the police cars disappeared down the road. Then Quint's cell barked.

"Quint here."

The voice from the other side of the world said, "How are things going? We haven't heard from you in some time. We have concerns about the short window you have to make those assholes disappear."

Quint didn't like being bird-dogged. "The mission will be completed around nine a.m. our time. You'll be reading about it in a special edition of the local papers sometime in the afternoon, along with a global Internet announcement of their deaths from a freak act of nature."

Chapter Fifteen

The Deluge

Quint suggested to the Jew, "It's time we got our ass back out to the cave. We want to be inside when the seawater spills into the meeting room. Witnessing the demise of the despots will be a pleasure. And if for some reason our scheme with the water doesn't work, we'll need to let loose a few grenades into the meeting room."

The Jew, who was still stinging from the police and coast guard visit, said, "I have a boat ready; it's at the dock now. I'm looking forward to the news coverage and the attention of the authorities being focused on someone else."

He ordered the warehouse driver to take the two Americans to the dock and drop them off, then wait for their return.

With the tide near its high-water mark, Jett and Quint surfaced inside the cave to see the water no more than an hour away from spilling into the mosque.

Looking at his watch, Quint remarked, "It's seven thirty. The water should dump on the despots in less than an hour. Let's take a look-see at who has arrived."

They crawled up to the perforated ceiling overlooking the room and looked down to see two of the world leaders who had arrived early arguing about something in their native language, unintelligible to the two observers due to the distance and the acoustics of the room. The water would soon find its way into the room and fill it to overflowing.

"It won't be long before these fuckers will know what it's like to have no choice but to try and die with dignity," said Jett. For all those they have brutally killed and tortured in the name of their "social justice, they will get the reward they deserve—being put in a position with no option but death. We'll see how they respond in the same situation they have imposed on others.

"My guess is they'll die like the rats they are, clawing and climbing all over each other trying to reach the last gasp of air before they inhale the seawater."

The other two heads of state entered the room and shook hands all around. It was apparent that each one in attendance thought he should be the spokesman and leader.

Quint remarked as they observed the collection of evil leaders, "They don't appear to be armed. I wonder if they have hidden handguns under their outerwear. It would be a shame if we performed our mission without an error, only to have these dickheads shoot each other. Then again, that would be an option."

The dictators were attired in the traditional dress of their countries of origin, except for the despots from South and Central America, who were wearing traditional Western suits. All were capable of hiding small handguns or knives.

Looking down on the assembled group, Jett said, "All we have to do is wait and hope Jake gets the door locked so they can't get out."

Jake looked over the balcony railing as the dignitaries arrived with their entourage of bodyguards armed to the teeth. The bodyguards were all eyeing each other suspiciously, not trusting the intentions of anyone within arm's length.

The dictators shook hands and dismissed their armed escorts, directing them to return to the mosque entrance, leaving only the guards provided by the holy site to stand watch over the meeting room.

Sensing it was time for him to sneak down the stairs and take out the two guards left at the entrance, Jake looked at his watch. It was pucker time.

Jake used the same volume of stun as he had earlier, and with all the stealth he could manage, he put a dart in each guard's neck. The first one dropped with a thud, alerting his partner, who turned to see what the noise was but didn't have time to do anything but grab his neck as the next dart found its target. He fell to his knees, but no warning came from his mouth.

Jake stepped over the bodies, hoping someone didn't come to check on things while the stunned guards were in la-la land.

Standing in front of the door to the meeting room, Jake turned the key to the right to lock the door, but it wouldn't move. He made a stronger effort to turn it, trying not to make any noise. It still wouldn't budge. *Jesus! What the fuck do I do now?*

Looking down at the guards, he could see he had little time to make his move, whatever it was going to be. The first one was moaning and starting to stretch. They would be out of their stupor within seconds.

Jake came to the only conclusion possible under the circumstances. He grabbed the key out of the ancient lock, opened the door, stepped inside, and locked the door from the inside. Then he bent the key in the lock opening and broke it off, thus blocking any attempts to open the door.

Just as he turned around to face the stunned faces of the assembled despots, the first splashes of salt water came pouring down through the caged ceiling.

Someone was pounding on the door. Jake pulled out his handgun and ordered everyone to be seated. They took their seats, but by the looks on their faces. he knew they would make a move on him before long.

To make the event look like an act of God, he didn't want to shoot anyone. But, of course, they weren't privy to the plan, and as they began to understand their plight, he might not be able to stop them from rushing the door without his being a surrogate for the Lord.

"Jesus Christ!" Quint punched Jett in the ribs. "Look! Jake just opened the door, stepped inside the meeting room, locked the door, and broke the key off in the lock. What the fuck is he doing? There will be no way out for him."

Jett looked down at the scene just as Jake pulled his pistol to keep the dictators in their seats. He could see that wouldn't last long as the water began to pour down from above. They would soon figure out their predicament and rush Jake to get at the door. "We need to figure out what the hell Jake is thinking. He didn't intentionally put himself in a no-win situation. There must be some plan to his madness."

Quint looked down as the water began to fill the room. His friend and fellow adventurer was about to end his life to save their mission. "Damn. He must have thought of something; what the fuck is it?"

Jett said, "The water is waist high and nearing the meeting tables. The shit-boys will start to panic anytime now.

The words had just left Jett's lips when the four world leaders surged as one towards Jake. He didn't shoot, but threw the gun at them and ducked under the table. They forgot about him in their stampede to reach the door.

The room was filling up rapidly, and in less than a minute the water was above the door. All the men could do was tread water and rise to the caged ceiling.

Quint, with the look of a person who had just seen the light of the Lord, exclaimed, "I have it! Jake is going to swim up with the water, and when he's close enough we can put the diving mask on him. He'll be able to breathe while the others drown.

"There's enough room to put the mask through. The only hitch is that when the others are dead, we have to deflate the buoys and let the water in the tunnel and cave recede. By the time we do all that, someone will have found a way to open the door, and the water in the meeting room will rush out with the bodies. I'm guessing Jake plans to ride the water down, and as the force of the water pushes everyone away from the entrance he'll grab the door jamb to stop himself. During the confusion he'll find his way back to wherever he spent the night, wait for the turmoil to settle down, and find his way out of the mosque. Piece of cake!"

Jake floated up with the others as the water rose towards the caged ceiling. He kept them at bay with his feet. Any chance for them to display some courage and dignity was wasted. They were terrified, climbing and pulling on each other to keep up with the rising water. It was a rewarding sight to see the fear in their eyes, the same fear they had watched when someone was executed in their presence. Paybacks are a bitch.

Looking up, Jake could see his cohorts waiting with a diving mask as he swam to the far corner of the caged ceiling. The others spotted him as he took the mask and began to breathe through it as the water flowed over his head, out of the ceiling and back into the tunnel.

Taking their last breaths, the despots swam underwater trying to reach Jake, but they couldn't hold out. One by one each sank back down towards the meeting table, his lungs filled with water.

Within minutes it was over. The mission was a success, but there was the little problem of escaping to tell the story.

While Quint was holding the mask for Jake, Jett began to deflate the buoys so the water could begin its journey down the spillways and back out to the bay.

Jett yelled over to Quint, "Tell Jake as soon as we get back to the surface, we'll head over to the mosque and give him a hand."

Quint had just relayed the message when the water began to rapidly recede, and Jake was on his way back down to the door, which someone had finally figured a way to open.

Quint yelled out to Jett as Jake slipped out of the diving mask, "The metal door has been breached. Jake is on his way back down to the meeting room floor. I hope he can grab onto something before he flows out with the other bodies. Jesus, there's nothing we can do for him from here. Damn! Let's collect the buoys and get the hell out of here."

With all the speed they could muster, Jett and Quint donned their diving gear and, dragging the rubber buoys, began swimming back through the tunnel to the cabin cruiser awaiting them on the surface.

As the water took him down towards the floor of the meeting room, Jake felt like a surfer riding the waves at Sunset Beach in Hawaii. He couldn't see the bodies, but he knew they would all rush out the doorway when the water found its only escape. He also knew that whoever opened the door had received the surprise of his life. The force of the receding water would take all in its path for an unwanted ride.

Jake would have very little time to grab something to keep him from following the others out the door. As luck would have it, his ankle got caught on the table, slowing him down enough to wrap his arms around the leg of the podium set up for speeches.

When the water had disappeared, Jake crawled out of the meeting room and returned to his perch on the balcony to watch for an opening to slip out of the mosque.

He'd been damn lucky and didn't want to push it. Time was on his side.

It was a good half hour before searchers could get back into the mosque to search for any bodies that hadn't already been found along the route the water had taken from the meeting room to the street.

The search parties of bodyguards and local authorities was frantic in their efforts, hoping to find some explanation for the tragic deaths of four world leaders in the ancient holy mosque.

They combed the area looking for clues as the bodies were being taken out. Two bodies had caught on the pillars holding up the roof of a passageway and were just being removed when Jake noticed that the steel door had been cut open with a torch. He wondered where the welder was now. The force of the water must have slammed the door into him and taken the poor guy for one hell of a ride.

Fortunately for Jake, everyone was looking down, not up. His position would be safe for a while, but eventually they would get around to searching the mosque from top to bottom. He hoped the others hadn't left any clues behind because the searchers were certain to be checking out where the seawater had come from.

His view from the balcony was ringside, just like a booth in Vegas for the dinner show, only this was serious shit. He sat there for a good two or three hours, watching the confusion below.

The floor looked every bit like an ant hill being stirred with a stick. Rethinking his position, Jake decided it might be a good time to get out of Dodge. With the disarray he could slip downstairs and melt into the crowd of people. It wasn't at all like the States, where there would be yellow tape around every death scene.

His clothes were almost dry, so he took a chance and joined a group of men who were loading the steel door onto a furniture dolly to be taken out to the street for a closer inspection in the light of day.

Looking up to the diving platform, Quint yelled, "Pull on the rope." A crew member on the platform caught the rope thrown by Quint, who, with the help of the deckhand, managed to land the first rubber buoy, with the second one not far behind.

After the buoys were aboard, Jett and Quint removed their diving gear for the short ride to the beach. Jett asked the captain to hightail it ashore, for they needed to help their friend at the Great Mosque.

The captain obliged, throwing the throttle forward and knocking everyone back on their heels. Even though he was skilled at the helm, dodging all the harbor traffic at full speed would require every bit of his years of experience.

He didn't need to wory about the huge wake he was leaving, for the entire coast guard and every other local authority were all at the mosque, along with every reporter from radio, TV, and all newspapers within a hundred miles. The event would make headlines worldwide.

The captain throttled back just in time to avoid plowing into the dock. His skill was evident, but scared the shit out of everyone on board.

Quint and Jett jumped onto the dock before the boat came to a full stop. They ran up the wooden ramp to the parking lot, where the Jew had an SUV waiting. The tires were smoking as the driver pulled into the main drag heading for the mosque, yelling, "Hang on, fellows."

Like the boat captain, the driver was skilled; despite the crowded traffic, they arrived at the mosque unscathed. It was mass confusion. There were ambulances, police cars, military trucks, and any number of government-marked vehicles. Fire trucks blocked the entrance to the mosque. Emergency personnel ran around in every direction. There were armed troops holding the crowds back. Limousines from all the embassies affected by the tragic deaths of their countries' leaders were parked helter skelter in the confusion of vehicles.

The bodies were lying near the mosque entrance, covered with their national flags. Ambassadors from the embassies were milling around, trying to identify their leaders, as TV cameras recorded the scene for the afternoon broadcast.

The chief of police was giving an interview as Quint and Jett exited the SUV in hopes of finding Jake among the crush of people. They wandered through the crowded street looking for him and listened to the chatter from the onlookers. Those that Jett could understand gave the impression that the tide had overflowed the mosque and drowned the leaders in a meeting room.

After checking out the crowd for an hour, they decided to step back to the seawall and just sit. They would observe the entire scene from the wall and wait for Jake to show. It was impossible to gain entrance to the mosque. They could only bide their time and hope he was okay.

Picking up his part of the steel door, Jake helped the others carry the door out to the street. Once they cleared the mosque entrance, the police directed them to put the door next to the covered bodies.

Jake was amazed at the huge crowd of rubberneckers and government personnel involved in the mass confusion surrounding the mosque. He tried to slip away from the group he'd hooked up with, but they were grabbed by an army officer and told to follow him as he headed back into the mosque.

Looking back over his shoulder he spotted Quint and Jett sitting on the seawall, but he didn't have the opportunity to get their attention. He'd tried the cell phone earlier, but the recent swim had killed it dead.

Not having any choice, he followed his recently acquired teammates back into the mosque to do the bidding of the army officer.

Once inside, the officer told them to stand by, that they would be searching the mosque from the main floor to the top of the towers.

Jett jumped up from the wall and pointed at the mosque entrance. "I think I just saw Jake. He was with the group that set the steel door down by the bodies, but then the group was directed by an army officer to head back into the mosque. Too bad we can't get in there to give him a hand. If that was him, at least we know he's ambulatory. Guess we'll just have to wait till he can take advantage of an opportunity to escape."

Quint suggested, "Maybe we could pass ourselves off as reporters for an American newspaper and bribe one of the soldiers to give us access to the mosque."

"Never mind, there's Jake. They've bound his wrists, and he's being escorted out of the mosque by the army officer. He doesn't look happy. I wonder what he did to gain attention to himself?" whispered Jett.

"Why are you whispering again?"

"Just that old habit kicking in, I guess."

The army officer guided Jake to the nearest military truck and put him in the cab, assigning a soldier to guard him.

Quint grabbed Jett. "This could be our best shot at helping Jake. Let's get over there and relieve the guard of his charge." He walked over to the SUV and explained the situation to their driver.

The driver suggested they mingle with the crowd, and when they were close to the army truck, bribe the guard to release Jake. He noted that the guard was not in the regular army and would probably take the money and disappear. Jake would be freed, and the army officer wouldn't have a clue what had happened.

Taking the driver's advice, Quint and Jett blended in with the rubberneckers, and when the crowd was abreast of the truck, they separated from the throng.

Jett walked up to the guard and produced a handful of American hundred-dollar bills. The guard recognized the universal value of the greenbacks. Instantly, his eyes grew very large and a slight smile reflected his greed.

Quint climbed into the truck with a big grin on his face and said to Jake, "You look like a drowned rat, my friend. What the hell did you do to have an army officer tie you up and escort you out of the mosque? Never mind; you can tell me later. Right now we need to get the hell out of here. This mob is trying to see the bodies, and they will be dispersed shortly. We need to be far away when that happens."

Quint cut the ropes, and they jumped down to find the guard running away with a fistful of Yankee greenbacks. Jett was smiling like he'd just taken a freshly baked apple pie from the farmhouse window. He led the way through the crowd back to the seawall and their ride.

The driver took his time, not wanting to draw any attention to their withdrawal from the mosque area. It was apparent the authorities were getting a handle on the situation, as the crowds had been moved back farther from the mosque. A roadblock was being set up behind them as they made their escape.

Pulling into the Jew's warehouse was a relief. When the door rolled down, it was as if a nightmare had vanished, and any further nightmares would be denied admittance.

The TV was blaring throughout the storage facility, announcing the demise of four or five world leaders due to a freak, unprecedented high tide that flooded the Great Mosque.

The entire warehouse crew was seated around the coffee station and TV when the three Americans joined them after a shower and change of clothes. There was a round of applause for their successful mission as they took their seats.

While everyone was watching the news about the mosque on the telly, Jett asked Jake, "Now, my friend, tell me how you came to be escorted by an army officer out of the mosque."

Jake was still shaky from lack of sleep and the harrowing experience in the flooded meeting room.

"Well, it went like this. I tried to get away when we carried the metal door outside, but he had another job inside and marched us back. As I was standing around with the rest of the workers, he walked up to me and started asking me questions. I didn't have a clue what the hell he was saying, and I didn't respond. This seemed to set him off, and he really got in my face. I pointed to my mouth and stuck out my tongue, trying to tell him I couldn't talk. He wasn't buying it and turned me towards the mosque entrance. He kept yelling at me as he forced me outside. That was all right with me. He was doing what I wanted. I didn't have any idea he was going to tie my hands and put me under guard. I was in the process of figuring out a way to escape when you guys showed up. It worked out well because we didn't leave any evidence that the freak of nature was man-made."

The Jew made his way up to the front of the gathering and announced, "Gentlemen, you have succeeded where formal governments have failed. You have reined in a collection of evil in one fell swoop. It's now time to gather your things. I have your jet fueled and ready for takeoff."

Without any further ado, the Jew herded the three into the SUV for the ride to the airport. He wanted to put distance between the hit men and their targets as soon as possible.

Quint's cell rang just as the jet's tires left the safety of Mother Earth.

"Quint here."

The voice coming through the cell from who-knows-where was calm and excited at the same time. He could hardly contain his obvious pleasure over the global headlines.

"Quint, you've accomplished the impossible. What your successful mission will mean to the free world is something that will have immediate effects and huge rewards over the years. A job well done. The board is pleased beyond imagination and has decided to double your fee."

"That's very generous of the board. Thank you."

"The board would like a face-to-face meeting when you arrive home. I believe there is a potbelly in the Far East who could use airing out. They may offer you another contract."

The cell went blank.

Quint shared his conversation with Jett and Jake, who were pleased to have the additional funds added to their accounts.

They shook hands and sat back to catch some much-needed z's on the trip home.

In the Name of Justice

"Mercy to the guilty is cruelty to the innocent."
Adam Smith

About the Author

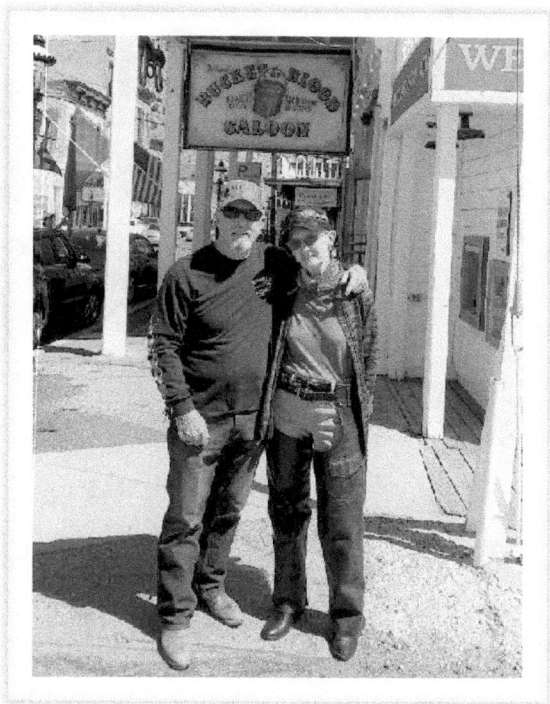

R. Michael Haigwood is a Marine veteran, life member and past Commandant of the Black Mountain Detachment, Marine Corps League. He worked on many construction projects as a member of the International Union of Operating Engineers, Local 12, from which he is retired. He is a longtime resident of Las Vegas, where he lives with his partner Jean.